Ivanni Delgado

Life Under A
New Perspective

Carmen

Life Under A New Perspective
Author: Ivanni Delgado

www.lifeundernewperspective.com

Library of Congress Control Number: 2013922962

ISBN: 978-0-9910720-0-2

$21.00
ISBN 978-0-9910720-0-2
52100>

9 780991 072002

Published in United States by Carmen & Son

Houston, Texas. www.carmen-usa.com

First Edition

I was barely an adolescent when, while walking through the streets of my native town, a middle-aged lady stopped me to ask if I was the son of Mrs. Carmen. To which I responded with much pride; "Yes, I am."

"I wanted to meet you, because she has spoken so fondly of her great son," she then told me.

"And how did you meet my mother?" I asked.

"Seven months ago, I was hospitalized in the capital where I knew no one. After having surgery they took me to my room and when I woke up I saw a woman greeting me with all the affection in the world. She had even brought me some fruit and magazines," she answered.

Very excitedly I said, "Thank you, thank you very much! I had never tasted apples, pears and grapes."

And that woman who appeared in my room asked me, "How do you feel?" and I answered, "A bit worried because..."

At that moment she interrupted me and said, "Did you think you were going to be alone?"

"Yes. I am from a small town very far from here and I don't know anybody in this big city," I answered her.

Then she told me, "I am from the same town."

I asked her, "How did you know I was here? I don't know you and I have never seen you."

She told me, "That doesn't matter. I think human beings should help one another and that is what I always do. Apart from feeling great pleasure in helping others, I think we should cultivate love amongst each other so the world can be more humane."

God!...that day when that lady told me all that, without a doubt, was one of the days in my life I felt the proudest. When that episode occurred, I was in junior high in a different city from where my mother lived. But thank God when I finished school I was able to move back to the capital with my beloved mother.

There I lived with her, without ever having a disagreement. Even though it may seem hard to believe there was never any argument between us. I understood then that love and respect together, was what made that relationship possible. My mother, for example, thought that no one should consume alcohol, but I did. Then I was able to understand that tolerating the imperfections of others is an indicative of the degree of love that we can feel for that person. And thus our lives continued. Until I decided to embark on the most interesting adventure in my life: coming to the United States of America to study.

I still remember when we said good-bye.

"God bless you son, everything will turn out well and you will have a happy trip." And so it was! My mother always dedicated the majority of her life to helping others. She was a much-loved person because of this. My mother never heard of the "Salvation Army", but she practiced the work of this organization for a long time. As a matter of fact, when I arrived in the United States and I found out about the existence of this institution, it reminded me much of her.

My mother would gather used clothes to give to the needy. She would gather it in the capital and then she would take it to our native town where she would disburse it among the people. Imagine the joy that was spread to the inhabitants of that town! It was a humble and very grateful town where my mother was always welcomed. The people in the town always carried her in their hearts.

I have never seen a soul with so much dedication to helping others. And I learned all these beautiful things from her. When I arrived in the United States, guess what? I became the foreign student who would pick up the new student. I would guide him and help him adapt to his new life. I helped give moral support to my classmates who sometimes felt homesick and wanted to go back home.

I remembered once I told someone, that returning home without having completed the mission was not right. To which my friend responded; "It's that I love my mother very much and I miss her so much that I want to go back."

To which I answered, "If you really love your mother, you should set yourself on achieving what you came to do and never appear before her with empty hands". That is what I would call love. The love of a mother should give us the strength to live and press on.

...And so just like my mother said, everything turned out okay in the United States. I finished my studies and returned to my town. But I no longer lived with my mother. I had already married and had a beautiful daughter. However, I remember always having the need to see her and worship her like no one else in life. My mother was definitely a very special person in my life.

I remember that in times of difficult situations, I would go see her, and without even telling her about my distress, after she blessed me, everything would change for me. I felt like that blessing covered my whole soul like a divine white light and I would recover all types of energy in my body so I could go on. After that, everything would come out right and would continue to come out right.

But of course, nothing in life lasts forever and unfortunately, good things come to an end. My dear mother decided to depart from the world of the living and she did it exactly at the time when there wasn't much to see in our town, but more importantly at the moment when her son could already walk through the paths of this world on his own.

At the cemetery, when we said the last goodbyes to my dear mother, in that precise moment, in a very spiritual conversation with her, I told her, "Beloved mother, you should feel very proud. You have done an immense work. You have helped people like you always wanted to. Today just as we are returning you to the earth from whence you came, I can tell you dear mother that your son is and will remain here to continue your divine mission. Here to my right I have my dear daughter; that like my other child, will continue my mission and yours also."

My strong desire for writing this book is to help people, like my mother would have. She always helped many people without even knowing them. I have wanted to continue her beautiful work, which I have done for some time now, by dedicating a part of my life to it. As a result, the objective of this book is to help people in the difficult task of living. To achieve this, it is necessary in our times, to make some changes in our way of facing life. For this reason, I assuredly think that the book should be titled *Life Under a New Perspective*, simply because this is what it is.

Table of Contents

Acknowledgement

I want to thank each and every person who has, in some way, been an inspiration for me writing this book. To all those authors who have written with the desire to help people, since my job is a continuation of theirs. To all those institutions like "Discovery Science Channel™", the "History Channel™" and the "National Geographic Channel™" which have served as a means by which to take the message of knowledge to the people. I would also like to thank my whole family for their support. And especially I would like to thank Milagros Hernández for her great support in the culmination of this book.

Introduction

Looking today at such a large part of humanity in the midst of so many calamities, and worst of all, so much hopelessness, I think it should be cause for an enormous reflection on the part of each and every one of us. We are a product of our thoughts. Everything we do whether good or bad is a consequence of them. That wise thinking of those men and women, who have brought us thus far, has disappeared with them. That thinking was logical, creative and positive, and it provided us a certain prosperity and happiness. We should have never forsaken such thinking; on the contrary, we should have studied it more in depth in order to enrich it.

Today, not being able to give an answer as to how it could be possible that our thoughts have darkened, we tend to believe that human thinking is being affected by some type of radiation to which we had not been exposed to in thousands of years. Perhaps our planet is moving through a point in the cosmos from where it absorbs radiations so strange that it has affected the way human beings think today. It seems that it is hard for all of us to believe what is happening in the world.

By trying to understand what is going on, we find more questions than answers. Thus we begin to wander until we reach a point where we embrace beliefs that far from helping us, they actually worsen our situation. Some people have come to believe that humanity's entire problem is due to the end of the world approaching, because this is what is written in the prophecies of them and those. In regard to these beliefs, a girl asks her mother:

"Why would God be permitting the destruction of his children?"

"It is that God is also getting tired of their stupidities," answered the mother.

The angels that God had sent to earth to protect and guide his people, had become indifferent and even sadder still: had turned evil. Today, we see them fighting and destroying each other, having reduced themselves to only a few. In one of those fights, the Angel Gabriel accuses the Angel Michael of having betrayed God. To which Michael responds to Gabriel in the midst of the altercation: "You, to please God, have blindly done all that he ordered you. I, on the other hand, have done all that God needs to continue with life."

In precise terms, it is imperative that we return to our thinking to become wise again and prosperous like we once were. We should see ourselves, and the world around us just as it is, without distorting reality so as to have a better perception of life. For this, it is necessary to reevaluate our beliefs. Conserving those beliefs that are rational or sustained by some evidence, for they help us to be open minded people, without prejudices and responsible for forging our own destiny, which will help us achieve our objectives. And eradicating those irrational beliefs without any support that limit our capacity to do and achieve things.

The problems that people confront today are a reflection of their thoughts; therefore to resolve them, it is necessary to adopt a more profound or advanced thinking, which consists of eradicating negativism and thinking more positively in a logical and creative way. Throughout the years our thinking has been deteriorating and has thus become negative. Our thinking makes us who we are. We will only be good if our thoughts are also good. People with thoughts directed towards prosperity will always end up being prosperous, just as people who think they are poor, will always be. Both prosperity and poverty are mental conditions. This is why we must direct our thoughts to what we want and they will take us there. It is time then to start living life under a new perspective.

It was with this in mind that I thought about writing this book, whose objective is none other than to help people in the difficult task of living. Because, believe me, life is not easy, much less with the wrong thinking. Living life under a new perspective is to confront and resolve our everyday problems, like our economic problems and our worries. By doing this, we will acquire a great sense of accomplishment. In order to continue through the long path of life, we should understand how we function physically and mentally so we can remain healthy and thus understand our emotions and thoughts, whose end is to put them to our service to achieve the correct attitude towards life, in order to achieve our objectives like personal happiness. This new perspective on life also includes, using the power of the subconscious mind to achieve all the good things to live a full life in a more humane society.

One of the motivations in writing this book surged when my neighbor from across the street came to see me to talk for a bit; something that we did regularly ever since I met him during hurricane Ike. When this friend arrived at my house, he asked me what I was doing and I told him I was writing. He then said to me, "I have never read anything of what you have written."

He then asked me to write about what had happened to him. I took that as a challenge and that same night I wrote his sad story. The following day when he saw it and read it with eyes tearing up, he said, "Thank you that is my story."

That first part of the book I called, "A Story of Faith", because after going through a difficult economic situation, this friend recovered thanks to his faith in God. Then I asked myself how many people have that kind of faith that would help them rise from such an adversity like that. The answer was simple; not many people. I thought that I could add to that story of faith a lot of knowledge so that people could turn it into wisdom and use it to solve their problems.

To achieve this objective of helping people in the difficult task of living, we start by presenting everyday problems, as well as their solutions. Then we will proceed to the knowledge of the incredible human body and the wonderful human mind in order to be and maintain ourselves in good health physically and mentally. To know our body and our mind helps us appreciate the things which we are capable of achieving, which in turn helps us develop faith and confidence in ourselves. With a healthy mind inside of a healthy body, full of faith and confidence, we can continue on the path to a better life. Sick we would not be able to accomplish anything. Ahead, we present the correct attitude towards life, which is necessary to develop in order to achieve a full life; this is why we say that life is a matter of attitude.

Up to now we have covered a lot of the important and necessary aspects to achieve a better form of living. Finally, we enter in full into what it is to live fully, achieving personal happiness with the support of the subconscious mind. We should transmit this happiness to others to have a better society, worthy of being a generation of change in order to continue preserving the precious human race.

The book contains five chapters, each one with five sub chapters. In the first chapter we will focus on the most important adversities that people face in everyday life: their economic problems and their worries. Also, we present solutions to manage these worries, acting on the positive worries and eradicating the negative ones, by the elimination of negative thinking and the cultivation of positive thinking. We also present the solution to prevent or overcome a financial crisis through a sound management of our finances.

In the second chapter we begin to present a series of facts directed towards knowing more about the incredible human body with the intent to be and stay healthy as our next step to continue forward in the search of a better way of living. Now, to enjoy good health it is necessary understand the formation of the human body, with its brain as the principal part. Also, to know the processes of renewal and aging that occur inside of us is to have a better idea of how to give more appropriate maintenance to our body. In other words, to keep it in good health, and in this sense vitamins and minerals can help us achieve this.

The presentation of knowledge concerning our body continues in chapter three. In it we center our attention on the wonderful human mind to truly appreciate the things it does. One of the most important products of the mind is our emotions, which we need to understand in order to manage and control them. The other great product of our mind is our thoughts, which make us who we are, thus to be better we must think more positively. Another fruit of the mind, of immeasurable value, is our intelligence. It is the key in taking us through the right path, with the objective of having a mind that generates good thoughts and ideas for us, and we should take care of it with good mental health.

Next, in the fourth chapter we cover the topics necessary for the development of a good attitude towards life, which will make easier the task of living. Life is a matter of attitude; for if it is good, we attain what we want. Now, to obtain a good attitude we must develop a good personality, positive beliefs and become a good friend. Moreover, in order to have the correct attitude in life and obtain the necessary things to live life to its fullest, people should also be optimistic, have faith and hope, develop a positive attitude towards money, have a good sense of humor and be free from bad habits.

And to conclude, in the fifth chapter we go through the aspects required to obtain personal happiness and with the help of the power of the subconscious mind we can acquire any other thing we may need so that we can ultimately live fully. In order to be happy you must want to be happy. Besides, the happiness we attain depends on our way of thinking. With positive thoughts and with the help of the subconscious mind, we can satisfy our basic needs, have aspirations, success, overcome our fears, and have a good partner in order to live a better life in the midst of a more humane society. In this type of society, we can all coexist without so many problems and secure our generation of change to conserve the beautiful world that is departing from us.

You can read this book whichever way you prefer, since it has no specific order. However, it is recommended you read the introduction of each chapter and subchapter carefully to understand what they are about and why. After finishing the book, keep it for future references and share it if you truly believe it's worth it. Every time you confront a problem in life or wish to achieve something, refer back to the book. I am sure you will find answers. Try to fully understand it so you can transmit it to others. Helping you, so you can help others is the mantra of this book and my hope.

1. The Everyday Life: Problems and Solutions

With the purpose of understanding our more common problems, so that we may overcome them and continue the path to a better life, in this chapter we will cover the issues of the everyday life of people, who sometimes reach economic collapse to the point where they must declare bankruptcy. We will also address all things concerning worries, not only of those which manage to liberate themselves from economic difficulties, but also all those that surge in each circumstance of our lives. Worries tear our soul without us realizing it, which is why we must attend them with great priority.

Given the importance that worries have in our lives and with the purpose of making possible the objective of this endeavor of helping people in the difficult task of living, we have presented a way of handling worries before their effects can lessen our quality of life. Also, with this same purpose we have proposed a solution to resolve or prevent a personal or family financial crisis through the good use of our finances. By learning how to manage our worries and our finances, we will have the greater part of the battle won in the difficult task of living.

1.1 A Story of Faith

Faith is the energy that helps us achieve anything, even overcoming a great economic crisis. For this reason, in this subchapter, I bring you the story of an everyday man, who I met during hurricane Ike while he was confronting an enormous storm of his own. He told me his heart-wrenching story of what had happened to him that led to his economic collapse. However, after the storm comes the calm and this friend saw the light at the end of the tunnel, which enabled him to lift himself up after being penniless. He was able to accomplish a better life for him and his family thanks to his faith in God. It is well to mention, that faith fortifies more when we also have confidence in ourselves.

After the Storm Always Comes the Calm

In the midst of an immense storm that pounded our community, I had the opportunity to meet this friend, who later told me his sad story. But like it usually happens, after the storm always comes the calm. This is a very optimistic phrase, but at the same time very real. The point is that in life, everything has a solution.

After the storm, I have seen how this friend was able to survive and slowly recover from having nothing. Interesting! Now, how many people pass through an economic crisis? Many! But, how many recover like him? Few! The big difference between achieving or not achieving things is our faith. Therefore, we begin this story of faith.

Hurricane Ike

God! I even remember that night of September 13, 2008 when winds of more than 170 km per hour pounded our beloved city of Houston, Texas. Hurricane Ike had arrived at around 7:00 o'clock that night. The trees around our house began to feel the sudden impact of the enormous gusts of wind and water. At the beginning, the trees tried to contain the force, but the fury of Ike was so strong that part of the leaves and the branches of the trees began to fall.

After a while, the trees seemed to have changed their strategy and they danced to the rhythm of Ike.

Sometimes it must be like this. We must first recognize what we are exposing ourselves to in order to confront it then. This way we will be giving ourselves the opportunity to be successful in combat.

The following day, around 7:00 in the morning, after a long night of vigilance, my daughter, my niece, and I went outside to see the damages that Ike had left. We noticed that 7 of our oldest trees had fallen, but not because they were old but because they were rigid and could not move to the beat of Ike.

We see that there are situations in which the more rigid you are the more fragile and weak you become. Therefore, the virtue lies in being firm and flexible. Now, this requires certain wisdom to know when to be firm and when to be flexible.

In the midst of this depressing scene I thanked God because the worst had passed and truly, our house and the house of our neighbors had not suffered greater loss. We saw that a limb from a tree had fallen on the roof of the house of our neighbor from across the street, making a hole through which water was coming into his master bedroom.

We almost always worry about bad things that might happen to us, something that is normal. But when we realize that we are not the only ones affected and that there are others in worse situations, our burden lightens. Without a doubt, shared grievances weigh less. Now, how do we know that we are not the only ones affected and that there are others in worse condition than us? Well we must simply communicate with those that share our surroundings.

A Sad Story

After assessing the damages and talking with our neighbors, as is usually the normal thing to do in these cases, we began to work as a team to help each other. Both of my next-door neighbors and I went to the house across the street to help repair the damage that the tree limb had caused on the roof.

We crossed the street and arrived at the house and there we introduced ourselves to Miguel, the owner of the house. After we repaired the hole on the roof, this friend began to tell us about the difficult situation he was going through. Miguel who is of Latin origin and a good Christian, is married and has four children. His wife takes care of the house and his children go to school.

After getting to know our neighbors from across the street, we determined that not only the calamity of Ike had devastated them, but that they were also confronting a very critical economic situation. However, from the furniture they had inside the house, you could see that they had had certain comforts. It was very sad when we heard this friend tell us that he was selling everything inside his house in order to buy food for his family. That was something very touching.

The human being is a very surprising creature, for it is always willing to help in tragic moments. That is its nature since it discovered compassion, thousands of years ago. One of my neighbors bought something that Miguel was selling, which helped him survive for more than 7 days. My other neighbor gave him some food and other useful things. I only gave him something of value, which he could use not only in those moments of desperation, but throughout his entire life: my friendship. Just like mother used to say, nobody is without God, for he always protects his children. Besides, God may be late, but he never forgets us. He is our guide and always presents himself to us to help us.

After hearing about Miguel's hardship, we were left dismayed. It is hard to fall after enjoying certain economic comfort. It feels like life is crumbling when we lose everything seemingly overnight. In those moments of anxiety and anguish, the mind is bombarded with a burst of questions as to why the situation occurred and not being able to find any answers, gives in to hopelessness. Once we come back to reality; seeing and accepting things as they are now, we see ourselves with the need to act in order to resolve the difficulty.

The story that this friend told us about the adverse situation he was going through, became even sadder when we saw that part of the cause of the problem was the deceit of a so-called "great" friend of his. The sadness mixed with the pain to form an immense feeling of emptiness, which also harbored anger. Miguel carried all that inside.

He told us that he acquired the house he now lived in with his wife and four children through this friend of his, whom he allowed to use his life savings and credit to purchase it. Miguel met this so called friend, when he offered free food at one of his Open Houses. This real estate agent also offered a thousand dollars to whoever could bring him a buyer. A tempting offer for someone who makes that much money in one month!

After a while, Miguel had brought several other friends into the business and they all purchased not only one but two houses. Everything was going beautifully. Miguel at that time lived in a very old house in Magnolia. But that was about to change, for this real estate agent would sell Miguel and his family two houses also.

After some time, Miguel began to notice that things were not right and the bank was demanding payment for the houses he had purchased. He then realized that he had lost all he had: house, car, his credit and even his job. Once he became aware of this horrible situation he had driven his family into, all types of aggressive thoughts assaulted his mind. He even began to feel hate toward the real estate man who had sold him the houses. He contemplated the idea of searching for him and making him pay. These thoughts remained inside of him for quite some time, but thanks to God and a pastor from church, Miguel managed to forgive him and let God do justice.

Some of Miguel's friends, including this real estate man, advised him that in order to get out of the situation he should declare himself bankrupt. At the end, after having accumulated so much debt and without any other option, he declared bankruptcy under chapter 13 in an attempt to keep his house. However, this situation with the house would take longer.

The important thing about difficulties is not how we get ourselves into them, but how we come out of them. In life, to make mistakes is human, and no one is exempt from committing errors. However, the importance of making mistakes is to learn from them so as to not repeat them. If we simply try to justify our errors or simply cover them up, we lose the opportunity to learn from them. In doing so, we would be doing much as the cat does. This little animal is very refined and aristocratic when it lives indoors, but when it lives outdoors its life is a bit more ordinary. The animal, after defecating, covers it up because it smells bad. This is what the majority of humans do when they make a mistake. The problem is that by covering up the mistakes, humans stop learning the cause of them and thus continue to make them over and over.

It is hard to face reality, but this is only one. When it comes, we must accept it regardless of how painful it is. When Miguel saw his wife and children, their faces reflecting their vast sorrow, he felt so much pain that it was extremely difficult for him to take it all in and he would go to his backyard and cry amongst the trees, and with his arms extended towards heaven; He would beg his God for help.

After everything came crashing down, Miguel could only turn to God. And with all the humility in the world he tells him: "Father, I know I did a lot of things that now I see were not right before your eyes, but Father believe me, I know you will, I simply wanted the best for me and my family and you know this Lord. Help me Lord; not to be evicted from this house with my whole family, not only because it is sad, but also because we have nowhere to go. God, my God help me!"

Is It Possible to Survive Only with Faith?

Although it may appear difficult, it is possible to survive only with faith. Miguel and his family did it and after three years, they still live in the same house. The bank made several attempts to evict them, but something always happened in Miguel's favor. Once the bank notified them that they had to move out, Miguel's son asked;

"What chances are there that we will be evicted?"

"Well, 97%" the father answered.

"Then we must hold on tightly to the 3% chance we have of staying," replied the son.

And apparently that small chance occurred. In one occasion, Miguel looked at his older daughter who was deep in thought. She stood before him and asked;

"Could it be that we will overcome this?"

"Yes, daughter", he replied. "We will overcome this. Something good is about to come. God will help us you will see."

With the help of the church and some friends, including me, Miguel was able to bring food to the table for his family. On various occasions he was forced to borrow money. He would ask a friend to lend him some for one week and then the following week he would pay him back with what he borrowed from another friend. He did this for some time and it worked.

Finally he was able to find a job as a machinist, doing what he knew, in a plant that built tools for the oil industry. With the little he could save and with the help of friends and his brother, he was able to buy a small used car, which allowed him to go from work to his home. In the meantime, he made new friends and looked for other opportunities.

The Light at the End of the Tunnel

In his search to try and better his economic situation, Miguel meets a friend who tells him about a multi-level company he just started. This company would commercialize a special product that contained an ingredient with medicinal powers. Without any experience in this type of business, Miguel decided to go along with this friend on the project. He had nothing to lose.

The sales from the business began to increase considerably. To the point that about 7 months later, Miguel was already making twice as much as he was as a machinist, which prompts him to quit that job and dedicate himself full time to the multi-level business . In a year, Miguel was already making five times more that he did as a machinist. Ah! He had already bought himself a bigger car in which the whole family could fit. By the second year, Miguel reaches the highest level of sales and receives and award as the best paid employee of the company and thus continues to rise in the following years.

1.2 Personal Economic Collapse

It seems like during the present crisis that grips the world; more people are prone to have an economic collapse. To help people avoid and or prepare for such an event, it is necessary to know what an economic collapse at the personal level is, what causes it and how the popular credit report can send warning signs about people's economic problems. It is also important to know how credit cards work and how we can use them so they can help us instead of cause us more problems.

What is a Personal Economic Collapse?

A lot of people have faced a financial crisis at some point in their lives, especially during this great economic crisis that has extended throughout the whole world. Whether the cause of the problem is a personal or family illness, the loss of a job or simply having spent too much; the truth is that a financial crisis on a personal level is always an exhausting and stressful situation.

When people's income is not enough to cover their expenses, they simply cannot pay their bills. They begin to receive constant warnings from their creditors, who having received no payment, turn over the unpaid bills to a collections agency. This exerts all kind of pressure on them until these people began to worry and stress for fear that they will lose their belongings, especially their house or car. This is how a personal economic collapse begins.

The way you manage a personal financial crisis to make it better depends on what caused it. If the situation was caused by over spending, the solution is simple; reducing your spending is sufficient. Now, if the cause is due to a personal illness and this prevents the person from working, or has caused additional expenses, then once the person regains his normal health; the problem should be fixed.

However, if the person is in a crisis because of the loss of employment and this was the only means of income, then the solution to the crisis will be more difficult, due to the fact that the person must first find a new job to improve the situation. The problem that presents itself in this case is that in an economic recession, like the one we see around the world today, it is hard to find a job and if you do, it will take some time, time which the person does not have.

The person in his desperation turns to any type of loan that he can get and ends up completely indebted. Some people sell whatever they can at whatever price they can get, and in extreme cases, they even sell their houses. If the person is single, perhaps this decision may not have much impact, but when you have a family, that decision of selling the house could seem as almost unthinkable. The house where we reside with our family, our home, should be sacred. When people reach these extremes, it is when they realize that they are in an economic collapse. A good indicator of the economic stability of a person is his credit report, which can show certain economic difficulties to the point of revealing the possibility of an approaching collapse.

Credit Report

The famous credit report is a detailed history of all the transactions of loans, credit cards, payments and non-payments of a person on the different types of open accounts under his name. The banks, financial institutions or any other company that issues credit or loans oversees all that information.

The report shows how the person handles the payment of his debts, if he always pays on time, or if he pays late or not at all. This report is given out by three very specialized agencies in the United States, which based on how the person handles his debt, gives them a score from 300 to 850. Any report over 700 is considered good. A bad credit report can be a sign of the economic difficulty and even an impending collapse.

Obviously, the report also contains personal information like personal facts, place of employment and residence, and indicates if the person has any legal sues pending, if he's been arrested or if he has declared bankruptcy. The credit report is of great importance in the United States. It is required of any person who applies for credit. It does not surprise me if soon someone will ask the person they want to marry for one.

Causes of Economic Collapse

In the last years, the cost of achieving a decent standard of living, having your own house and car, raising your children in a safe neighborhood and being able to give them an adequate education, has increased considerably. The majority of people live in an economically tight situation, to reduce their fixed expenses. In other words, those monthly expenses, that do not really vary from month to month, and are hard to reduce such as; the mortgage, medical insurance, school tuition, etc. This means that people have already started to eliminate or drastically reduce the unnecessary variable expenses like trips, entertainment, expensive clothing, etc. with the intention of keeping themselves off of the brink of an economic collapse.

There are various factors, which can cause or contribute to a personal economic collapse. Among them we can include; a divorce, the loss of a loved one, sickness, unexpected expenses, and decrease in income due to economic inflation or loss of a job. Each of these factors carries a specific weight in the structure of the family's budget, which is why we must act in a timely fashion in order to solve the situation. The worst thing you can do is ignoring them.

Divorce is a factor of destabilization, not only at the emotional level, but also at the economic one since it affects the family income. When both spouses work, after a separation, the family income will be reduced to only one and each person will separately pay their fixed expenses, which before had been shared. Clearly, this will last until another partner is found and then the situation returns to normal.

In the case of the loss of a loved one, the person may be affected mostly emotionally, even though; it could also have an economic impact, if that loss leaves a big expense to be paid. For this same reason, a sickness can also have a significant effect on the family budget. Now, if the sickness produces a long time or permanent disability, the family can quickly face a situation, which can imply the total loss of income or a portion of it.

In the regard to the actual rapid inflation over items of necessity like food, energy, public services, and the increase in the expenses of raising children, we can already see that our income, not even stretching it, is sufficient to face the basic obligations of everyday living. This is without including the expenses of car repairs, going to the doctor, or medical insurance rates, which have also increased. People's incomes are decreasing, but they do not realize this and continue using their credit cards with the same or more frequency and only pay the minimum amount, which adds an additional cost.

As far as unforeseen expenses, these can economically destabilize a person from night to day. The expenses of an automobile accident for example, where the insurance does not cover the medical treatment, can be massive and the people, having no other option, turn to their credit cards.

We see that the majority of people, especially in these situations, use their credit cards for everything. This is not the problem, but the fact that they have become accustomed to only paying the minimum amount at the end of each month. This is the biggest mistake that these cardholders can make. First, because they have to pay interest for the financing of the credit card debt and this interest is generally very high, and second; because the debt begins to accumulate until it becomes impossible to pay. The worst thing is that millions of people experience this situation, which leaves them in a difficult position in regards to the administration of their finances and to the decisions that help them overcome the crisis.

The loss of employment in itself represents one critical factor for economic stability. Now, it would be even worse if it is combined with other factors such as divorce, an illness, incapacitation, failed businesses, economic inflation, or an unforeseen expense. This catastrophic combination can become the trigger that can lead people to an economic breakdown and to declare bankruptcy, since the expenses of each one of these factors lessens the income of any one until they collapse.

Credit Cards

The most known credit cards issued by banks are VISA™ and MasterCard™. When you use these cards, the issuing bank finances your purchases and sends you a bill to pay within a month. Of course, these cards give people the option to make the minimum payment and charge interest on the financing of the rest of the balance not paid.

Apart from credit cards, we also have charge cards, the most well-known being American Express™. The main difference between credit cards and charge cards is that the first one can have a monthly balance to pay, subject to an interest rate, while with charge cards; the balance is required to be completely paid off at the end of each month. Charge cards in general do not establish a limit and the user must pay an annual fee for the card.

Another type of cards is the debit card, which is totally different in that no credit is involved. These cards function more like ATM cards. When you use them, the total of your purchases is directly deducted from your bank account. Debit cards are limited to the amount of money you have in your bank account, like when you use a check. Due to the limit on debit cards, and that charge cards require complete payment each period, it is the credit cards that can become the source for potential problems if not used correctly.

Use of Credit Cards: Solution or Problem?

Credit cards in themselves are not the problem. They can be a great solution if managed correctly. The problem is that the majority of the people have not learned how to use them correctly. Just like a weapon can save our life, but if we do not know how to use it correctly, it can also take it away.

The main problem associated with the use of a credit card is getting into the habit of only making partial payments or worse yet: paying only the minimum amount. *The secret is always to pay the total amount at the end of each month* to avoid the cost of financing and the accumulation of debt, which is really what generates the problem.

The credit card should be used as if it were a petty cash. We should only spend what we can replace. The big advantages in using a credit card are to use other people's money and at the same time obtain credit, which is of great importance in our actual life. To have good credit is to enjoy many privileges.

Another problem that presents itself with the use of credit cards is to ask for cash advances, which can become very costly, since credit companies frequently charge a higher interest rate with these advances than they apply to the financing of purchases made with the card.

Not understanding correctly what the credit limit on a card means can become another problem that leads a person into debt. If the limit on the credit card is $7,000 dollars that does not necessarily mean the person should spend that entire amount monthly, unless he can justify those expenses and pay them at the end of the month. People need to determine the amount that they can pay monthly according to their budget and use the card only up to that amount without caring about what the established limit is on the card. This practice will allow people to always make the complete payments, prevent expenses due to financing, prevent also getting into debt and enjoy the credit at the same time. This way instead of being a problem, credit cards can be a solution.

1.3 Personal Bankruptcy

Some people manage to overcome their economic collapse, while others, probably the majority, only see the alternative of bankruptcy as the solution. This is a decision that should be carefully studied. To make the best decision it is necessary to know what it means to declare bankruptcy, know the chapters that regulate it and its advantages, and also to know the aspects of the famous "foreclosure". It is of great importance to also know the process of recovery after bankruptcy, before making this decision. Personal bankruptcy is very serious and requires the evaluation of all the other available options in order to avoid it.

What is Personal Bankruptcy?

The majority of the people that go through an economic crisis, generally do not handle the topic of finances, neither do they understand their emotions and thoughts. Their confused mind cannot see with clarity any way out of the crisis and the worries begin. The stress, the anxiety, and the anguish drive the people, unfortunately to an economic collapse, which is usually followed by declaring bankruptcy.

The word bankruptcy has its origin in the Italian Renaissance. Back in that period, when a businessperson did not pay his debts, the process that would follow would be to break the bench in which he sat on at his business place. That is how the expression "ruptured bench" (*banca rota*), emerged which later on became bankruptcy.

In the United States, more than one million people declare bankruptcy annually, due to the accumulation of their debts, which have reached an unmanageable level. To the point that for them, to declare bankruptcy is apparently the only way they can overcome their situation. However, this option means that their credit history will be ruined.

In a situation of unemployment and with a debt that exceeds their ability to pay, people generally opt for bankruptcy. A high percentage of people are led to this option through advertising that does not clearly explain the consequences that are involved in the process of bankruptcy. Also, in many cases, not all the possibilities of refinancing the debt are explored, which is why it is recommended to consult with experienced people in this area before making the decision.

It is possible that this awkward legal process may end in despair represented by the weight of a debt impossible to pay, which limits a person if he would like to begin any economic endeavor. We have seen that with the actual economic crisis, each day there are less people not prone to suffer an economic collapse, which would make them unable to pay their debts. The problem generally surges as a result of unemployment, a major illness or too much spending. For some of these people, overcoming this crisis is a matter of time and a way of finding how to renegotiate the debt. For others, perhaps the majority, the only alternative is to declare bankruptcy. Before adopting this alternative, one should know its regulation, which is found in chapters 7 and 13 of personal bankruptcy.

Chapter 7

Two types of basic bankruptcy exist in the United States: bankruptcy under Chapter 7 and Chapter 13. Under both chapters, the cases should be brought before a federal court, which deals with issues of bankruptcy. Bankruptcy under Chapter 7, known as legal bankruptcy, requires the liquidation of all your possessions that are not exempt from the bankruptcy laws in the state you reside. The list of possessions exempt can include work tools and house furniture. Under Chapter 7, all your unsecured debts and unpaid accounts can be declared null.

Chapter 7 is the most common form of bankruptcy and it can eliminate the majority of the debts that are not exempt, which include: debts from credit cards, medical bills, the majority of personal loans, payments for traffic accidents and default of payment on vehicles. A designated officer of the court can sell part of your goods to pay your creditors. The people who file under Chapter 7 should wait 8 years before declaring bankruptcy again under the same chapter. A person is eligible to opt for Chapter 7 if they will not have sufficient income during the next 5 years to pay the 25% or more of their unsecured debts and lives or has properties in the United States.

After balancing the debts of the person, the court will notify him that his debt is terminated and finished, which means that he no longer is legally responsible for paying that debt. The process for finalizing bankruptcy under Chapter 7 takes approximately 4 months. It is important that if the person has a guarantor or co-signer in any of his debts, after his bankruptcy is declared; his creditors will contact his guarantor and will look for a way to recover the money that is owed to them.

Previously, 70% of bankruptcies were handled through Chapter 7, which in one shot eliminated all debts and the person started from zero again. However, the new law of 2005 makes it more difficult to file under Chapter 7. To begin with, it is no longer a jury who decides if the person can choose this option. Now his finances are subject to two tests: on one hand his income is compared to the state average and on the other hand it will be determined if by putting aside certain living expenses, like rent and food, these people can pay 25% of what is known as a "non-priority and unsecured" debt, for example the debt accumulated on credit cards.

If a person makes more than the state average and can pay 25 percent, he will not be able to declare bankruptcy under Chapter 7, which forces people to file under Chapter 13; which reorganizes the payment of the debt during a period of 5 years. Chapter 13 allows the person involved in the process of bankruptcy to conserve his mortgaged things, such as his house or his automobile that would normally be liquidated to pay off the creditors.

The new legislation concerning bankruptcy introduces two fundamental changes. On one hand it is no longer a jury who determines what the person can pay. Now, parameters established by the Internal Revenue

Service (IRS) are applied to decide how much to pay after deducting living costs. To protect his house, the person filing for bankruptcy must have lived in it for at least 40 months. Besides, if the person declaring bankruptcy has not lived 2 years in the state where he declared bankruptcy, he will only be able to file under the extension of the state where he has resided mostly during the 180 days prior to the 2 years. Other assets, which are protected, are savings set aside for the education of your children and accumulated 2 years before declaring and up to one million dollars in retirement benefits.

The new law also obligates the declarer to meet with a credit assessor during the six months prior to the filing of the bankruptcy and to assist financial administration classes. Lastly, it can introduce an element that can make it difficult to contract a lawyer to handle the paperwork. According to the norm, if the information of the filer is incorrect, the lawyer can be fined. This responsibility together with the additional paperwork required by the new law can lead many lawyers to be wary of this type of work.

Chapter 13

In the case of bankruptcy under Chapter 13, it is permitted for a person who receives a set and steady income to conserve certain assets, like his mortgaged house or car, which he would have lost through the process of bankruptcy. In these cases, the court approves a payment plan that permits the person to utilize future income to pay his debts within a period between 3 to 5 years instead of losing his assets. The waiting period established for bankruptcies under Chapter 13 is much shorter than the one for Chapter 7 and can last only 2 years.

Declaring personal bankruptcy under Chapter 13 is considered a reorganization of the debt. Under this chapter it is required of the person to pay a portion of the debt according to his possibility of facing a monthly payment lasting 3 to 5 years. Among the more common reasons for opting for Chapter 13 instead of 7 are: to be in debt with their mortgage and the payment of taxes or to try to keep their assets which the person would otherwise have been forced to relinquish under Chapter 7.

If a person declares himself bankrupt under Chapter 13, it is required of their mortgage company to accept their payment plan and they are given the opportunity to schedule their payment date with the creditors. In order to be eligible for bankruptcy under Chapter 13, individuals must live or keep properties in the United States, must have a steady income and have an adequate income at their disposal to pay the debts on a set payment plan.

One reason why some people choose bankruptcy under Chapter 13 and not 7 is because under Chapter 13 the person is allowed to keep all his assets in return for payment to their creditors, at least half of the minimum they would have had to pay if they had declared bankruptcy under Chapter 7.

It is true that declaring bankruptcy is a legal method in which one can better their difficult economic situation, but it is an option that should be considered as one of last resort. Even though debts can disappear after bankruptcy, it will always leave behind negative repercussions that will affect the possibility of obtaining future credit. Bankruptcy will remain in your credit report for 10 years and will complicate getting loans. It can also come to light in an investigation of previous jobs and can become an excluding factor for obtaining an insurance policy.

Without a doubt, bankruptcy is a hard blow for the people affected by it, especially in this current economic crisis where more than one million people have declared bankruptcy in the past year. The number of cases of bankruptcy has already reached an alarming level, which is why it is imperative to educate the people in this area to reduce the number of cases.

Foreclosure

Foreclosure is a legal process in which the financial institution, which gave a person a loan for the money necessary to purchase a house, carries out the repossession of the property for failure to pay. The laws on foreclosure vary from state to state. In about half of all the states, foreclosures constitute judicial procedures in which the financial institution presents a law suit against the borrower.

Unless the owner of the house can successfully counter the execution of the foreclosure, the financial institution will win the case and the house will be sold through judicial supervision to regain the amount of the loan. The foreclosure process varies in time, but generally it takes 3 to 10 months to finalize the foreclosure from the moment it is initiated.

One of the worries of the majority of the people is the ability to keep their house during bankruptcy. It is important to stress that the person should continue paying his mortgage on time during the bankruptcy process. It is also important to know that in a Chapter 7 bankruptcy, generally, the person does not manage to keep his house, nor stop a foreclosure. However, to keep your house under a Chapter 7 bankruptcy can be possible under a practice known as a "Homestead" extension, which under the terms of a Chapter 7 bankruptcy, permit a person to keep a portion of the value of his house. If this extension is the same as the amount the person owes on the house, he can keep it.

Recovery

After having declared bankruptcy, a person would have passed through a very tense situation and probably has had a traumatic moment. This person could even fear what this could mean to his future and could also develop certain feelings of guilt. The truth is, that it is something that can be devastating, which is why one should obtain all the emotional support from his family and friends and try to keep his head clear to be able to restore his financial health.

If the cause of the problem has been an unforeseen event, the person should assert himself to get it under control. If uncontrolled spending is the cause of the problems of his debt, he should try to make all the pertinent corrections so as not to repeat this mistake in the future. Regardless of what has caused their economic collapse, once the debts have been extinguished, the person should try to learn from the experience and try to better himself in the areas of economy and finances, to create a better financial future.

This implies acquiring certain discipline and planning for a better management of finances. Financial planning includes the setting of a budget to help control spending with respect to income. Keeping a budget puts the reality of finances on paper and keeps it in order for you to see.

Also, people who have declared bankruptcy and are on the way to recovery should keep their financial activity in a stable way, so that the credit institutions and their future creditors can see their economic progress, such as keeping a steady job and residence, paying bills on time, etc. It is recommended then, to start by staying in your present house and your same job for some time as a sign of economic stability.

A person should also open a checking account, or a savings account, if they don't have one. They should try to make them grow to show that they can administrate their money in a sensible way. It is important to use a credit card with discretion, without forgetting the advice on the management of credit cards in subchapter 1.2 on economic collapse. This will guide you on how to use your card, which will help you repair your credit. It is important to demonstrate to creditors that one utilizes his or her credit cards in an appropriate way and pays the entire amount on time.

If a credit card cannot be obtained because of a bankruptcy, one should try to solicit a prepaid or insured card. This type of card is given when you deposit money in a savings account in your bank, with a line of credit equal to the amount of money in that account. Think ahead about your future expenses, to better manage your money in a sensible way. Little by little you will rebuild your credit until you achieve complete economic recovery.

Some years will pass before you can accumulate savings and sufficient credits to be eligible for a mortgage, but if you have the will you can begin reconstructing your dream today. Consider planning for emergencies. If you have reached your limit and are not able to pay your debts, or if you have crossed the line and reached bankruptcy, you know how events in life can dramatically change your financial circumstances.

Start saving and make it a goal to save enough money to cover at least the expenses in case of an emergency. With persistence and discipline, you can reconstruct your credit in a period of 3 to 5 years. Most likely, it took some time to find yourself in this financially critical situation, but with a plan and some discipline you can not only reverse the situation, but you can make it better than ever before. For this, it is recommended that you study all the topics mentioned in subchapter 1.5 on personal or family finances.

1.4 Worries

After having gone through a difficult economic situation, to the point of collapse and personal bankruptcy, people are left with many worries. It is clear, these worries not only occur due to economic problems, they can always occur in any aspect of our lives and they do not need any special event to make an appearance. They affect our quality of life by limiting our capacity to achieve our goals and move forward.

Worries are part of our culture as well as of ourselves. This has made us perceive them as something normal. But herein lays the issue. While we don't see them as a problem, we will do nothing to resolve them. These worries live inside of us, tearing our soul without us realizing it and will continue to do so until we do something to prevent it. In order to deal with worries, we must really understand them; know what they are and how they come about; what are the most common types of worries that we face and why we worry. Once we know this, we can finally control them to prevent their devastating effects and continue in the path to a better life.

What Are Worries?

Worries are feelings of restlessness or alarm that we have when we are faced with certain situations that we think could have a bad outcome or that can cause us some harm or injury. The legitimate objective of worries is to reach positive solutions with respect to the dangers in life, by anticipating the risks before they happen.

Worries, like all other emotions, are signals transmitted by the emotional brain over an uncomfortable situation or problem. They are composed by one or more thoughts associated with feeling of fear and distrust. As long as we have these types of thoughts, we will also have worries.

When worries indicate that we face a problematic situation that requires a solution these serve as an alert to analyze the situation. Look for possible solutions and act accordingly. In this case, worries fulfill their function and are considered positive and necessary.

Therefore, worrying is simply the mechanism that our mind utilizes to find a solution to whatever uncomfortable situation that one may be going through. Once the problematic situation is resolved, the worry should disappear. We see then, that worrying is very normal, since it can help us anticipate dangers and even prevent them.

However, when worries are not attended correctly in time to resolve a problem, they will continue reappearing over and over, which increases the intensity of the worry thus producing anxiety. Unattended worries will persist and may even become chronic. This is where the problem arises. We should take care of each one of our worries and resolve the uncomfortable or problematic situation and that's it; the worry is over.

The classic example of attending a worry occurs when we are driving our car and a light comes on. Uh-oh! If we look at the dashboard and see that we are running out of gas, we look for a gas station, get gas and the problem is solved. Now, if on the contrary, the person does not pay attention to the sign and tries to ignore it, his worry will continue intensifying to the point that the person tries to hit the dashboard as a result of their distress and can end up running out gas and end up stuck with an even bigger problem.

When worries lose their legitimate objective of alerting us to act out and solve the problem, they are considered negative and unnecessary. These worries are the ones we should try to eliminate so they cannot cause us all of those difficulties. When worry becomes a habit, we live in a constant state of tension, which affects our way of perceiving the people and the world around us, without us realizing it. We end up worn out from the stress and from all the problems associated with it from a mental breakdown to psychological disorders.

Types of Worries

There can be different types of worries, the most important ones being rational or irrational ones, depending on the cause which produces them. This cause can be real or imaginary. Now, the degree, intensity, and duration of the worry, does not depend on its cause, but on our perception and the evaluation we make of the situation, which can in turn depend on our way of thinking. This ultimately complicates the topic of worries generating other types of worries.

Rational and Irrational Worries

If the worries are based on a real cause, then they are known as rational. If on the contrary, they are based on the imagination, as is most commonly the case, then these worries are considered irrational.

A rational worry can be positive in the sense that it helps us realize that something in our life requires our attention and it prompts us to act so we can analyze and solve the problem in an appropriate way. On the other hand, an irrational worry has a negative impact since far from helping us solve the problem; what it does is aggravate it. Faced with an irrational worry, we imagine the worst situations; ending up trapped by anxiety without searching for any solution to the problem.

We end up focusing with more frequency on the negative aspect of worries, giving greater importance to the bad things that could happen to us. We live then unconsciously with certain fear, which lessens our capacity to focus on the necessary aspects to solve the problems. Negative worries are unnecessary and debilitate us and wear us out physically and emotionally.

Positive worries only last the necessary time it takes to help us find a solution to the problem and act. If there is no solution or the problem is out of our hands, worrying is unnecessary. If we do not act and we stay submerged in the worry, it would be like always tripping on the same spot. The people that live are the ones that continue advancing, while the ones who are constantly tripped up are the ones that die.

Negative worries are produced by our repeatedly negative thoughts, which cause us restlessness, anxiety or fear, but do not lead us to a solution. They simply stay in our mind, feeding themselves and compounding our physical and mental discomfort, which will ultimately end up altering our behavior.

Negative thoughts are a result of processing distorted information by the brain, which make the world look more dangerous to us than it really is. This is because that distorted information is not based on reality. Negative thoughts are not easy to eradicate because they form patterns of thinking so automatic that they become a part of our life that we are not usually conscious of.

Other Types of Worries

Besides rational and irrational worries, there exist other types of worries that I would call worries of force majeure cause, of external cause, of past cause, and of future cause. As you can see, each day we invent more worries. These types of worries can even become rational or of real cause, but negative and unnecessary like irrational thoughts, which are why we should always avoid them.

Worries of force majeure cause are those that although they affect us directly, their solution is not under our control. Such is the case of the political situation in our countries. The current political leaders are taking the world through a path that is far from prosperous and healthy. To feel worry about this, would be very legitimate, but what we should not do is continue worrying because the solution is not in our hands. We can vote to elect politicians for public offices, but only in countries with true democracy, can we change something.

Worries of external cause are those that simply are not ours. The problem is somebody else's. When I began to study at the university, one of my professors invited me to eat at a restaurant famous for its steaks. He ordered a big steak and I ordered the same. I ate my entire portion, like a good boy, but he left almost half of his. I thought: what a waste... I asked my dear professor if he did not feel any worry about all the people in the world who had no food to eat, to which he answered, "Worrying does not solve the problem."

He continued saying that "if I ate all the steak, it would help even less". Then he said, "Furthermore, there are more possibilities of helping if you leave some on your plate, because in some way it could be reaching the hungry people in the world. Do not think about solving world hunger. It is not in your reach and it will only bring you frustration. Besides, that problem is somebody else's. But if you can help one hungry person, then feed them. You will be in good standing before God and you will not generate any worry."

Worrying about others is very common among us. This tendency in humans to help our neighbor emerged when our forefathers developed compassion. Something which is very beautiful, but what we should not do is to allow the problems of others to become negative and unnecessary worries in us. If someone we know has a problem, if we can help him or her solve it, that is good, but if we can't, we should not add another worry to our life.

Worries of past cause are those that refer to regrets for actions that we took in the past. We worry thinking over and over about mistakes we made as if by worrying could amend them. This creates a feeling of guilt that increases our stress even more.

Worries of future cause are those related to the uncertainty of tomorrow. Worrying about these situations is not useful for they only increase our difficulties. When politicians in the hopes of winning an election invented the story of global warming, in which life on this planet was on the verge of disappearing; more than one third of the children in the United States lost their hope of living in a beautiful world. That worry will affect them in their future lives and could even be passed on to their children.

God! We worry about everything. If there is nothing to worry about, we make something up. But people do not always worry about the same situation, nor do all people worry in the same way when confronted with the same situation. Worrying will depend greatly on how we think. We better make sure our thoughts are directed in the right path.

There are people who think that worrying is their responsibility and that the more they worry the fewer the possibilities that something bad will happen. Others believe that worry motivates them to act. We learn to worry as children, watching our parents doing it constantly, later those worries become a habit very difficult to break.

When my neighbor from across the street was going through that difficult situation, the worry he felt was rational because the cause was real. Worrying helped him realize that he and his family were going through a crisis and that he needed to do something to resolve the situation. That forced him to go out and look for a job, and in less than 7 months he had the matter resolved.

Now, let's say that this friend also would have imagined that perhaps one of his children or his wife would get sick and he would have no money to take them to a hospital to make them well or that they could die from hunger and it would be his fault...and on and on, his imagination could have thought up a number of things. In this case, the causes for worry would have been imaginary and would have only intensified his worries. Maybe he would still have not resolved the situation and maybe he would even be sick.

Why Do We Worry?

We all worry. Around 40% of Americans worry each day and in the majority of them, the worries are chronic. We worry about almost everything, about our relationships with other people, about the economy, about our health, about our job, or our studies and even about our own worries. Now, where does so much worry come from? Well, we learn them from adolescence, from our parents or from traumatic situations from the past.

In normal conditions, we worry to resolve a problem that is making us uncomfortable. Once the problem is resolved, the worry should cease. However, this is not always the case. It is here where the problem with worries begins. Some people believe that worrying can help them prevent bad things from happening to them, or prepare them for the worst that could happen. The people who worry a lot can come to generate a series of beliefs on worries that can end up creating a kind of myth in regards to their concerns.

The people that think this way generate negative thoughts, which only serve to further aggravate the problem of worrying about worries. These people treat these negative thoughts as if they were real. The problem is that the more they think that their negative thoughts are real, the more they will have to worry. Perhaps the saddest thing is that they come to believe that all the bad things that happen to them is their fault. Moreover, these people become intolerant of failure. As a consequence, they develop a horrible feeling of guilt and an immense fear of failure, which puts an enormous limitation on achieving the things they desire. With so many worries accumulated in their minds, these people believe that it is necessary to resolve them immediately and they treat each one of their worries as if they were an emergency. They become impatient and even act with ineptitude.

Frequently we worry more than we believe. Our worries become a habit and we even come to consider that worrying is something good to do. We think that we should worry because it is the only way we can resolve our problems and because it is a way of avoiding greater difficulties or dangers. By thinking like this, we feel good worrying which incorporates worries as normal and part of our lives. This will make the task of ending worries much more difficult.

The habit of worrying provides a reinforcement in the same sense that superstitions do. Given that people worry about a lot of things that have very little probability of occurring in real life, they become so influenced as to believe that something magical like a charm can protect them from any harm lurking in their future.

Management of Worries

We should manage our worries in a way that allows us to have certain control over them and thus avoid the adverse consequences they can incorporate into our lives. The best way to manage our worries is by following these 5 steps:

1. Analyze Our Worries

2. Act on the Positive Worries and Eliminate the Negative Ones

3. Accept Unnecessary Worries as a Problem

4. Eliminate Negative Thoughts

5. Cultivate Positive Thinking

1. Analyze our Worries

To analyze our worries we must clearly define what worries us, see how probable it is that they will happen, and identify the thoughts that accompany the worry. Once we have identified the thoughts associated with each worry, we should try to eradicate the negative thoughts and only conserve the positive ones. In the same manner, we should determine the type of worry and proceed to resolve it, if its solution is viable. If not, then we should try to eliminate it.

2. Act on the Positive Worries and Eliminate the Negative Ones

When we are confronted with a positive worry whose solution is under our reach, then we should immediately act to resolve the uncomfortable situation, just as we saw in the section "What are Worries?" It is important to remember that when we do not attend our worries on time and in an efficient manner, these will become repetitive and chronic, which will, as a consequence, generate problems of anxiety, stress and depression; besides maintaining the habit of worry.

To eliminate negative worries such as irrational ones, worries of external cause, of past cause or of future cause, etc., we should first identify and then analyze them as described in step 1, so we can later eliminate them one by one. To eliminate worries of past and future cause, we must always live in the present. The present is simply the division between the past and the future. If we pretend to live in the past, we will always live worried, anchoring our lives to events that already happened and can never be changed. Trying to correct our mistakes made in the past is to waste all our energy pretending we can change the past. On the other hand, if we pretend to live in the future, we will live full of all the uncertainty caused by not knowing what will happen tomorrow, which would produce more worries in us.

We can use the knowledge of what has passed or what we did in the past to help us predict future events. After all, life is a cycle. Events repeat themselves over and over in various places and different times and thusly life continues. Not to know history, is to be condemned to repeat its errors. We should know history, not to live anchored to the past, but to learn about the future.

3. Accept the Unnecessary Worries as a Problem

As we have already said, worries are part of us; this has made us see them as something normal. This is true until the worries become an obstacle in the carrying on of our lives. At that point, our worries become a problem and we should accept them as such in order to find a solution. Otherwise, until we don't see them as a problem, we will not do anything to resolve them and they will continue to stay with us.

4. Eliminate The Negative Thoughts

In order to eliminate negative thoughts, we must first identify them so we can later retrain our brain to generate better thoughts. Although it may not seem easy, it is, with the help of our subconscious mind, as we will see in chapter 5.

Our thoughts generally arise automatically. They can be positive or negative and almost always start with an internal conversation with ourselves, or what we commonly call, talking to ourselves. That internal conversation is an endless amount of unexpressed thoughts, which pass by our mind each day. Some of those internal conversations we don't even pay attention to.

Also, this internal conversation can indirectly generate parallel thoughts. For example, a person can be thinking about his first plane trip and develops a conversation with the mind itself, with many details about the things he has heard or what he imagines about the trip. If what he is thinking about in his internal conversation is positive, there is no problem, but if he suddenly thinks that he heard that someone he knew had lost his luggage when he went on a trip, this parallel thought will scare him a bit, but he will continue his internal conversation on the positive aspects of the trip until the conversation ends. Later, that negative thought of fear that he can lose his luggage, can emerge when he is not even thinking about the trip. Each time that thought surges, the person feels fear.

In effect, after the trip, he loses his luggage and generally the person will always say, "I knew it! I knew it!" Someone with a logical thought could ask,

"If you knew it, why didn't you avoid it?" Obviously, the answer of the effected person would be, how? To answer this question, first let's try to understand the why of the situation.

As we will see in the section of how thoughts function in the mind on subchapter 3.3, each thought has as a result, a positive or negative action depending on the type of thought. Now, for that action to take place, the thought should pass from the conscious mind to the subconscious, which after lodging the thought, will try to convert it into an action, as is explained in subchapter 5.2 on how to use the subconscious mind. Thoughts can pass to the subconscious automatically when the conditions are present. This happens without us even realizing it. How can we avoid those negative thoughts from lodging themselves in the subconscious, allowing it to convert them into action? Well, simply by eradicating those negative thoughts.

Let's take the example of the luggage. Each time that a thought emerges that the luggage will get lost, we will ask our subconscious for that not to happen and we will reinforce it with affirmations and visualizations. In other words, we affirm mentally that the luggage will arrive and we will imagine that they will be dispatched and will arrive at our destination to be picked up without any problems. When we no longer worry about the negative thought over the luggage, it is because that thought has been eliminated. For more detailed information on how to utilize affirmations and visualizations, please refer to the section on how to program the subconscious mind in subchapter 5.3. Once we have mastered that training we will have a great tool to eliminate negative thoughts and avoid losing our luggage.

If the thoughts that cross our minds are mainly negative, it is because we have a pessimistic vision of life. Pessimism only leads to failure, which is why we should eliminate negative thoughts in order to have success in life. Now, how can we know what types of thoughts cross our minds while we think? We must simply, listen to our mind and concentrate on what we are thinking to know its content. Following is a simple way of detecting negative thoughts.

If a person is always highlighting the negative aspects of a situation and gives less importance to the positive aspects, that person thinks negatively. Other characteristics of people with negative thoughts are: they always blame themselves each time something bad happens; automatically anticipate the worst; always see things as just good or bad, or black and white. In this sense, for these people there is no intermediate solution. They always think that everything has to be perfect or otherwise they are a failure.

The following example best illustrates the case of a person with a negative thought. A young man went out with his girlfriend for the first time and they went to a beautiful lake in the midst of dense vegetation surrounded by wild red roses. They traveled the entire lake on a canoe, fished, ate, drank and made love. After 7 hours, the girlfriend says that it is time to return to the hotel.

The boyfriend, despite all the beauty of the date, only thought about the fact that his girlfriend had told him that they had to return to the hotel. He thought something had not turned out right, that it was his fault, that his whole week had been ruined, that no one wanted to be with him, that he did nothing right and that he was a total failure. My God!

The reality of this case is that it was a wonderful date and that the couple had enjoyed themselves, but for the boyfriend, the reality was that the date did not end well. We can see that his negative way of thinking has distorted reality and the worst thing is that it brought him suffering. It is possible that he will breakup with his girlfriend and thus continue living his miserable life, when in reality, he should have been happy if he had thought positively.

5. Cultivate Positive Thinking

To cultivate positive thinking is simply to encourage this type of thoughts and turn away from our mind those that are negative. Thinking positively means to confront adversities in life in a more positive and productive way. It is to think that the best is yet to come. If the thoughts of a person are mainly positive, that person is optimistic.

Positive thinking has a great effect on our lives, including our health. Among the benefits that these types of thinking produce in our health are: a more useful life, less depression, less levels of difficulty, better management of stress and problems. Thinking positively allows people to confront better stressful situations, which reduce the harmful effects of stress on our health. Optimistic people tend to live a more healthy life.

A positive person simply highlights the positive aspects of a situation and gives less importance to the negative aspects. He does not blame himself if something goes wrong, always has hope that everything will turn out right, does not go to extremes and understands that things do not have to be perfect; there is room for the intermediate. They also understand that not all things in life turn out like they would like them to, and even if they did, we should confront life as it is, with all its ups and downs. If we benefit from a problem, or strengthen ourselves in the face of adversity, or prosper in a time of crisis, and finally convert a calamity into an opportunity, then we will be thinking positively. To think positively, we should believe more in ourselves, since we have all it takes to be successful.

The Effects of Worries

Worries are the central cause of anxiety and depression. Fifty percent of the people in the United States have confronted serious problems of anxiety and depression sometime in their lives. The worst thing is that these problems have continued to increase in recent years.

Excessive worrying can cause major problems that can go unnoticed. These unnecessary worries affect our health, leaving our body vulnerable to stress, anxiety, and depression, just to name a few of the most common problems. These worries also affect our intellectual capacity,–preventing us from making good decisions in order to adequately resolve our problems.

If we don't confront them for what they really are, a problem, we will never resolve them. This would bring as a consequence, worrying over our worries themselves, which would keep the worry alive. This definitely aggravates the problem even more. Finally, these unnecessary worries will end up affecting our relationships with other people in our environment until they undermine our quality of life.

In moments of economic crisis like present times the majority of the people live from worry to worry. Now, if we add to our worries over our health, interpersonal relationships etc., an economic worry, this can cause our bag of worries to collapse. Not being able to count on sufficient resources to continue with a normal life, increases exponentially the problem of worries in people.

One cannot be productive in everyday life when worries dominate our thoughts. They simply absorb too much energy.

This economic crisis that politicians have led the world into has caused millions of working people to lose their jobs. Perhaps the worst of all, is that it is very difficult to find a job. Imagine how worrisome life could become, when even those who have their jobs are worried about keeping them. They also worry because galloping inflation has caused their salaries to no longer be sufficient for anything. They are also without the opportunity to begin a new business, since loans have become so hard to come by. No one is investing, and the economy is stagnant.

People's minds nowadays, are filled with one worry after another. Their worries are constant and produce anxieties in them. As the worries become repetitive and chronic, their anxiety intensifies, also becoming chronic. This could generate in them a loss of control and emotional disorders like: a mental block, nervousness, panic, phobias, rages, obsessions, and a limitless number of negative things. These disorders could cause them to abandon common sense, when thinking about things that perhaps may never happen. They will end up developing a negative thought, which would alienate their mind from a *logical and positive thought*. Besides, that entire negative attitude, which is the product of so many worries, can unleash a series of illnesses, which have worries as a common factor in them.

Almost all people that suffer today from serious illnesses like aids, cancer, arthritis, etc. are people with chronic worries. These people cannot stop worrying. Some of them believe in worrying as a way of confronting the possible threats and dangers that surround them and even believe it can calm their anxiety. Unfortunately, the solutions to problems do not surge from negative worrying. On the contrary, the mind block out thinking repeatedly on the same worry, and this ultimately ends up generating fear.

The people who suffer from chronic worrying end up seeing dangers and things no one else can see. The worry can turn itself into a mental addiction. We can see clearly that excessive worrying does not lead us to anything good. The only way to help resolve the problem of worries is to adequately manage them in the way we discussed in the previous section. Otherwise, the worries will wear us out, not motivate us and lower our productivity as our emotional energy is lowered and finally ends up increasing our levels of anxiety, stress and depression.

Anxiety

Anxiety can be defined as the condition of a person that has experienced a commotion, restlessness, nervousness or worry. In some cases it may only be a normal emotion necessary to survive since it alerts a person to risk. When a person is confronted by an anxiety situation; the body increases the production of certain chemicals, which levels were below the normal before such situation. This augments his faculties of perception.

However, beyond normal, anxiety can become a disorder in people who cannot control their worries. As a consequence, in order to prevent anxiety from becoming a problem, we must control our worries. The disorder of anxiety generally develops slowly. Usually it starts during adolescence or youth. The symptoms can become better or worse at different moments, and frequently worsen in times of stress. Among the symptoms of people with an anxiety disorder we have the following: they worry too much and can't control their worries, they have problem concentrating, get agitated easily, have sleeping problems, they develop tremors or nervous tics and become irritable.

An anxiety disorder can produce panic attacks or phobias. The response that anxiety generates in a person is to flee from or fight with their fear. Now, when fear paralyzes the actions of a person, it becomes a phobia, which is a sudden reaction where the person loses control of the situation and tries to flee from it.

Another disorder associated with anxiety is anguish. Even though normally it is believed that anguish and anxiety are the same thing, this is not so. The effects of anguish are greater than those of anxiety. Anguish can produce blocking reactions, paralysis and inhibition; while anxiety causes reactions of panic attacks, desires of fleeing and agitation.

Stress

Worries produce anxiety and stress. Just like worries and anxiety, normal stress helps us in our survival. But in excess, it ends up making us ill. Now, who does not suffer from stress in these times? Traffic generates stress, also the noise, the economy, contamination levels, and our job. Almost everything stresses us, even enjoyable things like social reunions or group diversions.

People who suffer from a high level of stress are more susceptible to suffer a heart attack, a stroke, cancer, psychiatric problems, etc. Stress also accelerates the process of aging. It is necessary to improve our control over our worries in order to stress less. We should dedicate more time for enjoyment and relaxation, since our personal achievements would be useless if our stress does not allow us to enjoy life.

After controlling our worries, one of the most effective tools to help us reduce our nerves and maintain control of our stress is a deep breath and relaxation. It is also recommended to take vitamin C and B complex, together with a mineral like iron for women and zinc for men. This combination of vitamins and minerals is what is known as the anti-stress formula. It is important to control stress, due to the fact that it enormously affects the organism and lessens the intellect, even in people of high intellectual efficiency. Besides, worries, anxiety, and stress generate negative thoughts capable of plunging any person into depression.

Depression

Excessive and unnecessary worries can produce depression. When people worry incessantly over something that cannot be resolved immediately or over a worry that has become repetitive and chronic, an emotional excitement is generated in the mind that also remains unresolved.

Once the emotion is generated, it should be calmed or deactivated to complete the biological cycle of excitement in the circuitry of the brain. If the calming of that emotion is not completed during the day, then it will continue at night during your sleep. This will cause people to require periods of sleep more intense than usual in order to deactivate those unresolved worries, which normally are both mentally and physically tiring.

In these cases, sleep is not a repairer like it should be in normal conditions, since the brain spends a lot of time trying to calm the worries that could not be acted upon or resolved in any way during the day. This brings as a result, great weariness at the end of your sleep.

Waking up tired, after sleeping for hours is synonymous with worry, as is, waking up too early in the mornings. This abnormal awakening occurs as a kind of mechanism of survival for the brain which feeling tired, tries to wake up in order to rest. When the person wakes up feeling worse than when he went to sleep, energy and motivation is lost. Thus starts the cycle of depression and as a consequence, the feelings of hopelessness, tiredness and apathy, which later appear, giving the already depressed person more to worry about, and only worsens the situation.

Depression is a disorder of your state of mind, accompanied by discouragement and unhappiness, which can be transitory or permanent. Among the symptoms that depression presents we find; prolonged sadness, decline, irritability, and an impaired sense of humor and loss of interest in regular activities that were enjoyed before.

Depression can have detrimental social and personal consequences in the everyday life of a person through a poor professional or academic performance, deterioration in family relationships, as well as with any other social ties. It is necessary to attack this problem once its symptoms start.

Depression can be caused by multiple factors among which we must emphasize worries and stress. However other things also cause depression: sentimental problems, loss or accidents involving our loved ones. Depression can also be caused by the consumption of illegal drugs or alcohol abuse. In conclusion, to avoid falling into a depression, we should attend its causes as we have already seen. As to the consumption of drugs, we will address that topic in the section "Free from Vices" in subchapter 4.5.

1.5 Personal and Family Finance

We have seen a detailed story of faith about a person who experienced an economic collapse and bankruptcy and thanks to his faith, was able to come out of the crisis. However, all the suffering caused by the worries of going through that situation could be avoided by making a good use of our finances. In order to have good financial health, we should learn to have discipline in our finances by spending only the necessary. We should also plan so that with good financial management over our finances, we can achieve a stable and comfortable economic situation. For this, we need to create and faithfully keep a budget that will allow us to cover all of our expenses and still be able to save. We can invest part of our savings and stay economically stable.

Avoid Economic Collapse through the Good Use of Finance

As we endeavor to examine the causes that produce a personal economic collapse, we can see that the most influential factors are the external ones related to the economic environment and in a lesser degree those factors associated with people. The external factors include the changes in the economy of our countries, which produce inflation with its respective decreases in salary. Apart from this, a stagnant economy does not produce sufficient jobs and even puts at risk the already existing ones. The internal factors include a serious illness of a person or of someone in his family circle and some important unforeseen expenses that can alter the budget.

From what we have seen in ordinary everyday people, it would seem that to them the factors in the cause of an economic collapse are out of their hands. This would lead them to think that no one is exempt from collapsing economically. However, this is not entirely true, since there are ways to avoid a collapse. Bad financial management is the real reason why everyday people fall into economic problems.

A great deal of people lack financial knowledge, while the other part does not, but because of laziness does not utilize it. Of course, in neither of the cases, exists any excuse not to adequately manage their finances, since a lot of knowledge is not required to be financially healthy.

Now more than ever, we must prepare ourselves in the good use of our finances, to combat the imbalances that government introduces to the people in our countries' economy by turning them "upside down". It would not be fair to see governments undermine our finances without us doing anything about it.

It seems that governments have become some kind of executioners of their own people, when trying to introduce economic policies not compatible with the way of life of people, furthering them from prosperity. Policies so confused that sometimes not even the governments themselves understand and worse, don't seem to care about. How can they understand what the working people are going through, when many of those governors don't even know what it means to have to work, in order to put bread on the table to support a family?

Now, worrying about government's actions would be legitimate but unnecessary, as we mentioned before. We have no control over it. Therefore, the wise thing to do is to be prepared in order to protect ourselves from the economic imbalances, continue maintaining our family and keep going on with our lives. One of the actions that we should immediately take is to develop good financial management with good planning. There is no other alternative.

The management of personal finance starts with the management of your checkbook, which has been since its implementation in the XVIII century, a fundamental instrument to administrate funds in a checking account and thus pay for our purchases or for services we receive. The checkbook, besides the checks, also includes a small book to write down the transactions in the form of deposits or payments that are made during any period of time.

If the record of the transactions is kept accurately, we can at any moment know how much we have left in the account and obtain better control over our money. This way, we can avoid writing a check with no funds, as well as, avoid spending more than what is in the account. At the end of the month, we reconcile the checking account with our account balance from the bank.

Balancing our accounts is the first step in the task of managing our finances better.

We can see that if we learn to manage adequately our checkbook, we can then keep a healthy administration of our wealth. But this, however, has been precisely the fundamental problem in the bad management of personal finance. People have not given the necessary importance to the managing of their checkbook, due to laziness more than anything else. It becomes, therefore, totally imperative that we dominate this first step in the adequate management of our personal finance to later begin to develop financial discipline.

Financial Discipline

Everyday people commonly feel that money evaporates and at the end of the month have no idea what they did with it. The main problem of people is that they spend more than they earn, which leads to a situation where they can't pay their debts until this becomes unbearable. In order to overcome this problem, people must become conscious of what it means to manage themselves with financial discipline.

Financial discipline in general terms is to maintain certain rules with respect to the management of our finances in order to reach a certain level of financial health, especially in terms of spending what we earn and the savings we can have. It is very important to learn that we have to make money before we can spend part of it, not all of it. We should discipline our spending and develop the habit of saving. Of course, for any type of discipline to achieve its objective, it must be accompanied with firmness, consistency, and perseverance.

As far as spending goes, it is necessary to develop the habit of spending on what is necessary and at the right price. The person should make an analysis before any purchase to determine if what he is buying is necessary and has a fair price. For this, he must first ask himself if he really needs what he is going to buy; otherwise, the intent should end there. But, if the answer is positive, he should proceed with the next question: is the price of what I am buying fair? If the answer is yes, the purchase takes place. Otherwise he will continue the search for the best item that he needs at a best price.

Of course, the analysis is done mentally and with time, as it is practiced, our subconscious mind will do it automatically. Once the analysis has been implemented, the person will spend only on what is necessary and at a fair price. A woman will then no longer be seen buying a purse more expensive than a dress, or a man purchasing a tie more expensive than a suit.

We should develop the habit of not buying things solely on a whim or because they announce it on television, or because we saw it on this person or that person, or simply out of compulsion. Compulsive buyers always end up buying more things than they need. We should try not to buy things when we are under emotions. In this sense, it is necessary to educate economically ourselves, and our children. In other words, not let ourselves be manipulated by our feelings or our children's feelings, since we end up buying things only for indulgence. A lot of the things that are bought out of indulgence are not even useful and quickly end up in the garbage can.

Another very important habit to develop is to always buy solutions, never buy problems. For example, if we buy a car, whose maintenance is more expensive than what we can afford, then we would be really buying a problem. We should also develop certain priorities for spending. We should not buy a vase when we still need to pay the electricity.

A very distorting factor in financial discipline is any vice that a person has like smoking, consuming alcohol or illegal drugs. Generally, these expenses are more difficult to control, which is why it is of great importance that we keep those vices under control. The large majority of people with these vices always end up having economic problems, unless they can generate a good amount of income.

Financial Planning

When my daughter, Ivannia, had finished high school she told me she wanted to study System Engineering.

"How come?" I said.

"It's what the rest of my classmates are going to study," she replied.

I advised her that she should choose a career that she could master without any problems. She answered that she wanted to be an engineer like her father. The biggest difference was that her father felt an immense passion for mathematics, while she, on the other hand, didn't like it that much. This could cause her certain difficulties in the pursuit of an engineering degree. Very intelligently, she admitted that she should change her major and chose Business Administration, a career that she culminated with success.

Parents should help their children choose a career based on their strengths to avoid setbacks, and so they can enjoy the beautiful stage of going to the university. In this sense, I did the same with my son Ivanni. This without a doubt is planning. Now, does this have anything to do with financial planning? Yes, definitely. If the right career is not chosen, our children could take longer in graduating, which would mean unexpected strain on the finances on the part of whoever is paying for the education of the kids, which generally is the father.

Once my daughter became an administration student, I opened her, an account in a bank with sufficient funds to cover 7 months of expenses and I asked her to take charge of the administration of her funds. I explained to her to try to withdraw only the monthly allowance unless it was an emergency. In that case she could withdraw enough to cover an emergency, but she would need to replace that money in the following months. I also told her that for every dollar she saved, I would give her another one as an incentive to save.

The first month was a disaster because she spent way more, to which she claimed she had to help her grandfather. To this I said, just the same; you need to replace that extra expense since that is what we agreed to. Perhaps at that time she did not understand that I was only trying to discipline her. Having overcome this inconvenience, she once asked me to meet her so we could talk about something very important. She told me that she needed a raise in her monthly allowance because it was no longer enough for her. When I asked her why it wasn't enough, she took it the wrong way and was annoyed. I told her to make a list of all her expenses so I could analyze them. It was at that moment that she knew what her expenses were and how much they added up to.

Together, both of us analyzed each expense and determined which ones could be reduced and which ones couldn't. Little by little she was learning. However, I once called her and I could tell that the telephone company had turned off her phone service for not paying on time. After they hooked it up again, she called me smiling and told me that she had forgotten to pay the phone bill. Maybe I was a bit harsh with her and I told her if she had been the administrator of my company, that act of negligence would have cost her the job. Her laughter turned to tears, but till today, she never forgot that and she learned to meet all her obligations.

The training continued and each time she learned more how to manage herself and she didn't get annoyed as much. About a year later, she asked me to take her on a trip to which I answered no because she first needed to learn how to cover her basic living expenses and food, something she managed to learn also. Before graduating, she mastered the management of her finances. She already had a car, a place to live and she traveled with her father throughout the American continent.

Financial planning consists in setting goals that can be achieved through the use of good financing. However, typically everyday people live their lives without any planning. This should change if we want to avoid economic adversities. The greatest difficulty that people confront in this modern world is on economics, the other problems that we face are much easier to resolve. For this reason, we should give financial planning all the importance it deserves. In order to have prosperity we not only need to make money, but also know how to administer it and for this we need to plan what to do with our finances.

People should not live to work, but work to live. Now, living should never mean to work to have an income that allows us to only eat and dress. Living is much more interesting than that. Life is beautiful, and for that reason we should be prosperous to generate enough money to meet all our obligations and those of our family. We should also generate sufficient money to save and invest in order to increase our wealth and help our own.

When that point is reached, great peace and happiness is felt. Life under this perspective makes more sense for it would lead us to living it fully.

Let's therefore, start planning. Normally we initiate into the working world as teenagers, after we finish junior high and with minimum wage. But, because we generally still live with our parents, it will always be enough, since they pay almost all of our expenses. In our first job we should have a very positive attitude about the job, as well as, towards the company that has given us the opportunity.

The goal of teenagers should be to make enough money to pay their next level of education: high school or college. By this, not only do they free their parents from one more burden, but they start to become independent economically speaking. When teenagers reach this goal, they have trained themselves in financial management, acquiring a great sense of responsibility, which will prepare them for the next stage after graduation.

A college education helps us increase our income and have credit, which we need to learn how to manage correctly. In the United States, credit is very important in all aspects of economic life. As we have already seen in the section on the use of credit cards in subchapter 1.2 on economic collapse, we must appropriately manage our credit cards and for this we must use them only to buy or pay things that are within our budget. When we receive the balance, it should be paid in full. You should never finance expenses on your credit card. This bad practice had led many people to have financial problems. For this reason, 70% of the population of the United States today find themselves with debt problems.

People with university degrees should be earning at the end of their first work year around $5,000 dollars monthly. If this is not so, then this should be their goal. This income is considered currently in the United States an *optimal salary* since it permits people to live with certain comfort after paying their basic expenses like their personal expenses, transportation and housing and still be able to save a small part of their salary.

With this optimal salary, one can already start living well. The majority of the people start to buy things, cars, houses, etc. However, the first thing one should do is save. Always remember: you have to make money first in order to later spend a part of it and still have some savings left which is closely tied to our economic stability.

Before investing money, first it has to be earned and before investing in other things, we should invest in our peace of mind. To achieve this objective, one must save until he has accumulated a fund equivalent to 7 times his monthly salary. Once he has accumulated these safety funds, this should remain so that he can always count on it. With this idea or practical rule, a person can have certain peace in case he loses his job. During this period of 7 months, exists all the possibilities that one can find another job, while the funds from his savings allows him to cover and continue his normal life during unemployment.

For those people who for some reason could not get a university degree, the goal is the same: try to achieve monthly incomes around the optimal salary to assure the beginning of a better life. And of course, continue the recommendations previously mentioned on savings. By taking advantage of their talents, many people, with the correct dedication and attitude towards work have achieved this. A university degree helps, but it is not essential to obtain economic well-being. The difference would be that without a university degree, it could take longer to achieve the goal of earning the optimal salary. However, the great thing about the United States is that there are opportunities for all to achieve their dreams.

At around 27 years old, young people will be thinking about marriage and starting a family. This age is good because one starts to mature and define what one wants in life, besides at that age one should already have acquired certain economic stability. The ideal thing would be that the couple could have earnings equal to or greater than the optimal salary before getting married and thus be able to enjoy marriage before having children. That first stage of marriage, and perhaps the most beautiful, has to be enjoyed above all.

If, after a certain time, the couple considers that they are sufficiently responsible, that both are good for each other and that it is well and worth it to have a child, they should keep in mind that this decision is going to affect their economic situation. To compensate for the impact, the couple should generate an additional income of minimum wage for each child they decide to have. Let's look at our finances to have a better idea of what we should be spending.

As a practical rule, the total expenses of a family should be about a maximum of 90% of their earnings in order to save at least 10% religiously. The approximate total of the living expense should be about 30% of the total income, while the total expenses of transportation should be about 20% and the total of the family expenses should be about 40% of the total income. According to this practical rule, a family that generates and income of $5,000 a month, can spend $1,500 a month on housing, $1,000 on transportation, plus $2,000 in family expenses for a total budget of $4,500 and still this family can save about 10% or $500 dollars.

The expenses of a family of $2,000 dollars include food, health and medical insurance, clothing and entertainment. This of course, is not including a child. Some people do not care about the economic considerations we have mentioned, and they allege any excuse to have children any way. However, we should always try to be responsible parents and bring our children in this world when we are capable of supporting them and giving them an adequate education to guide them towards prosperity.

Planning gives us control over our future and the future of our loved ones. For this reason, we should plan all we can to avoid distortions in our finances. Each time we take part in any activity in our lives this will have an economic impact. Good financial planning starts with the implementation of a budget, which is very easy and any person can do it and keep it.

The Budget

The personal or family budget is an essential key element in the financial planning of a person or of the family, for this constitutes the tool that will control finances, through the utilization of money in a responsible way, without spending more than what is earned and still be able to save part of the income. A budget offers, at the end of the month, a balance that shows the difference between what has been earned and what has been spent. If the earnings supersede the expenses, the person is capable of saving. These savings can be put away to invest later or be used on some unforeseen expense.

A well-made budget serves to show us what we spend the money we earn on, to follow up on the expenses and be conscious of them. Also, it keeps us from throwing our money away, helps us save, and gives priority to certain expenses in order to eliminate or reduce the least necessary ones. With these savings, we can accumulate a fund dedicated to emergencies and be able to face unforeseen expenses like an illness, a car breakdown, or the loss of employment. Savings can permit people to live peacefully and according to their own possibilities.

If expenses supersede earnings, the monthly balance will be negative. This could happen in some months and be compensated for in others, but never should become a routine. If this situation lasts during several consecutive months, then the savings will be depleted and the people will normally resort to credit to pay their bills. That is why it is important that at the first moment this imbalance occurs, the necessary corrections be made to avoid falling into that same situation which places economic stability at risk.

The budget should include all income and all expenses, as you will see in the example on the following chart. Among income should be included: wages, bonuses, extra jobs or any other income received. While the expenses should include: living expenses, transportation and family maintenance as well as any other expense we have not mentioned here. After subtracting all the expenses from the total income then we should have the results of our total savings.

Living expenses include the payment of rent or the mortgage, if you own your property, as well as insurance payments; the respective public services like electricity, gas water, trash and any other repair or maintenance expense. Also included are the communication expenses such as: the telephone expenses whether they are fixed or cellular, Internet, etc.

EXAMPLE OF PERSONAL/FAMILY BUDGET

INCOME	Balance $
Salary	5,000
Other Income	
Total Income	**5,000**
EXPENSES	**Balance $**
Living	1,500
Rent	
Mortgage	
Insurance	
Public Services	
Communications	
Transportation	1,000
Vehicle	
Monthly Payment	
Insurance	
Maintenance	
Other: Bus, taxi	
Personal or Family Expenses	2,000
Food	
Health and Medical Insurance	
Clothing	
Entertainment	
Other Expenses	
Total Costs $	**4,500**
TOTAL SAVINGS $	**500**

In regards to transportation expenses, apart from the monthly car payment, car insurance and maintenance are also included, as well as, gas, service and repairs. In the case where a bus or taxi is used as a means of transportation, whether it be do diminish expenses or because there is no car, then those should be included in the section "Others: Bus, taxi" of the transportation expenses.

Personal or family expenses include: all the expenses related to food, health and medical insurance, clothing and entertainment. If your budget allows it and the person wants to continue his education, those expenses can be managed under a new category of expenses, which can be called "Education". Education expenses include all the expenses of tuitions of the family whether it is the parents or the children, books and any other school activities. Any student loans can also be included in these educational expenses.

If you do not have all the available information necessary to write up a budget, you can use estimates that are as accurate as possible and make adjustments along the way as you execute the budget. You can also use the practical rule, which we spoke about on the previous section. This way total expenses should be 90% of total income and 10% should be saved. All the living expenses should be 30% of total income, transportation should be 20% and the total group family expenses should be 40% of the total income.

At the end of the month one should have a bit more information in regards to his or her personal or family budget and better yet at the end of the year, which would allow them to come up with a more realistic budget to improve their finances. Then an individual can adjust the practical rule cited previously and personalize it according to his lifestyle. The importance of estimating is to have some information to go on. All the sciences have been initiated in this way, by trial and error.

To evaluate the budget, we need only to see if it is serving its purpose, which is to make sure the income covers the expenses and still leave us something to save. At the end of the period that we wish to evaluate, the execution of the budget indicates to us how well we have carried out our financial planning. Of course, if we follow the guidelines of the previous section, we would end up paying our expenses and saving a treasured and desired 10%. But, do things always occur like that in real life? Definitely not, we can end up paying for things that were not in the budget and end up with a certain imbalance.

The interesting thing would be, not how we fell into that expense outside the budget, but in how we will manage it from there on to avoid it from distorting our budget in the future. We can also make all the adjustments in respect to the expenses. Of course, there is not much we can do with fixed expenses, since these do not tend to vary much from month to month and they must be paid, like the mortgage or any other rent and the car payment.

However, we can reduce those variable expenses even when they are necessary expenses like water, gas, electricity, phone, food, clothing and transportation, if a more moderate use of them is made. There are other expenses that are not as necessary like entertainment and even certain types of clothing, which could be reduced without any problem. Once the necessary adjustments are identified, the budget needs to be elaborated again and kept faithfully.

Currently there are many ways to make and keep a personal or family budget for an easier management of finances. If you don't want or can't have the most sophisticated tool, I recommend that at least you convert the budget example presented here into an Excel document. You can also download a personal finance application from the Internet.

Savings and Investments

As we have already seen, before we can spend money, we must first earn it then save it to invest part of it. With savings, one can create an investment fund. This fund should be the total saved in excess of the safety fund, which we already mentioned is equivalent to the savings of 7 times the monthly salary and which should be permanent. The investment fund can be set apart to cover emergencies or unforeseen expenses or to accumulate enough capital to make an initial payment on an important acquisition such as buying a car or a house. It can also be used to cover the costs of the couple's education or the education of a child, prepare the person for retirement and to make any other type of investments. The more one saves the more options for investment one has and the more control he can have over the future.

Against these investment funds, a person can make loans without paying interest, as long as the loan is for covering emergencies or unforeseen expenses and it will be replaced or adequately paid back as soon as possible. In other words, instead of applying for a bank loan, or asking someone else for the loan, you give yourself the loan. But if you want to go to the bank, the majority of them have representatives that can help you with loans and even show you how to enter the world of investments and explain the different types of products available to obtain loans and to invest.

After people manage to accumulate safety funds, as we have already mentioned, everything they manage to save above this fund, including the interests the bank pays is set aside to create an investment fund with which one can make the two basic investments of a person or family, buying a car and a house. However, before making this decision, one should check to make sure that the investment fund has sufficient money to cover the initial payment required for the acquisition; likewise, the total income should be checked.

If the income of the person or the family is above the optimal income, which currently is $5000 a month, there should be no problem, since this is sufficient to assure the monthly payment of the two acquisitions previously mentioned and even continue without any economic restriction. Now, if the total income is under the optimal, it is recommended to first buy the car and after paying it off and your income can guarantee the monthly payments on a mortgage, then buy the house. The important thing is not to acquire any debt that cannot be paid later. For this reason, it is recommended to set as a goal to have an income equal to or greater than the optimal income. One way to increment your income is to speak to your employer and see if he can give you a raise. The other is to find a part time job on the side. If one manages to get any one of these options, it is very important to maintain the spending constant in order for additional income to be set aside only to satisfy what one wants to buy.

With the intention to make the investment on the car and the house more productive, it is important to know that a new car can usually go 7 years without a problem, as long as its respective maintenance plan from the manufacturer is fulfilled. For this reason, it is recommended to buy a new car, if and when possible, keep it for 7 years then sell it and buy a another new one. On the house, it is recommended to refinance the loan when the opportunity presents itself like for example, when the mortgage interest falls one point under the interest agreed when the debt was acquired. In situations of high inflation, when our savings are not earning enough interest to compensate the effect of inflation, it is recommended, if you have the money, to make payments on the principal of the mortgage or pay it off. People should not live to pay mortgages.

People should capitalize the increments on their income. In other words, get benefits out of them. To do this, it is necessary to maintain the same level of spending. After acquiring your car and house, with the balance accumulated in the investments fund, people can make other investments like buying stocks, bonuses, fixed term deposits, certificates of deposit or CD, etc. The people at your bank can help educate you on these types of investments.

Up to now the types of investments we have considered are of little or almost no risk, but with a low interest rate. After taking the previous step, if there is still sufficient capital in the investments funds which is available, the person can invest up to 27% of the available balance for investments of greater risk (but of greater gain) like starting their own business, buy an existing business, or associate with others. Even in this, the person should continue to have a safety fund and in his investment fund less the 27% invested. Also, it would be desirable for the person to keep his fixed income.

Because of the winds that blow over our world economy, each day it will become more difficult to find a job and keep a roof over our heads. To face those challenges and promote prosperity for one's family, responsible parents should, as part of their planning, leave their children a roof to live under and a business where they can work and of course, a will in their family's name, in case something should happen, so that the family inheritance will not pass into the hands of the state. This would be the ultimate goal of personal financial planning.

Generally speaking, people start to make money after they are 41 years old, like Colonel Sanders and many others. By the time they are 57, people should be free from debt and enjoying life. There are many wonderful people that have spent half of their life trying to make their money and the other half using it to help others. Thanks to the investment of many of them, a lot of us, the people, today can count on a job that grants us a prosper life; hoping someday we could be one of them.

2. The Incredible Human Body

In the previous chapter we were able to learn about the more important difficulties of everyday life, like our economic problems and our worries, as well as, their respective solutions. This has only been a step in the long road to achieving a full life. However, that puts us on the right path. To continue ahead, our next step should focus on being healthy and keeping ourselves in good condition. This is the matter of this second chapter. We need to be in good physical condition since being sick will not get us very far. Now, to enjoy good health it is necessary to know our incredible human body, as well as to know what we can do to keep it in shape.

In this sense, we should begin to understand how our body is conceived and formed; how our brain functions and matures; to know the processes of renewal and aging, because of what interesting they are and what they can teach us about ourselves. And of course, the other part we must know about our body is how to keep it in good health and how vitamins and minerals can help us achieve this.

2.1 Formation of the Human Body

The sexual union of our parents, one man and one woman conceive us. Out of all of our father's sperm only one manages to penetrate the fertile egg in our mother. This single sperm, like all the others, contains in its head 23 chromosomes, which unite with the other 23 chromosomes in our mother's egg to form the 46 chromosomes of the human genome of a baby.

Inside each chromosome are the genes, which contain hereditary information of the mother and the father. The sperm unites with the egg to form a living cell. The human body begins to form with a fetus that develops inside the womb. This period of formation of the body is comprised of 9 months, in which one simple cell evolves until it forms a child ready to be born.

Child body is formed by small organs perfectly designed, which constitutes a miracle of nature. Each one of those organs is made up of thousands of millions of cells functioning in a highly orchestrated way. These cells are the building blocks of life and we have about 100 million of them in our body all working in perfect harmony to make us who we are.

Inside each cell is found a molecule known as DNA or deoxyribonucleic acid. This molecule is the one that gives instructions to each cell on how to grow and what its functions are. DNA is the chemical blueprint of instructions on how to create each new life and is unique in each person. The DNA molecule is capable of duplicating itself thereby, transmitting the information on hereditary characteristics from cell to cell and from generation to generation.

Once the baby is formed, it comes out of the womb and enters into a new world, the world of people. It is here where he starts his walk through life, the most interesting journey of any person. When the child is born he faces his biggest difficulty, having to choose between life and death. In other words, he has to breathe or else die. His lungs had never breathed before because they were filled with amniotic fluid, which protected him during the nine months of pregnancy.

So the newborn runs the risk of drowning. But his body also comes equipped with an adrenal gland situated above his kidneys that sends a great influx of adrenaline around the body, bringing the lungs to life. The muscles that we need to breathe immediately begin to convulse and thus we take our first breath, which constitutes perhaps the most important breath of our entire life. During our lifetime, we will breathe about 700 million times.

Our lungs pump air without stopping each second of our lives. This air quickly passes through the trachea, then through thousands of ramifications and reaching about 30 million sacs of air called alveoli, which deposit oxygen in our blood and ejects the carbon dioxide we exhale with each breath. The alveoli perform this work constantly while we are alive.

Barely a few hours after being born, we know and understand nothing about the world that surrounds us and solely depend on our instincts to breathe and to eat. Newborn animals are in better conditions to survive than us humans. If it were not for our mothers, the majority of newborns would perish. It is because of this, that it is believed justly so, that our mothers are the greatest forgers of humanity.

Maternal milk apart from feeding us also protects us. Once outside the womb, we are exposed to a world full of invisible bacteria, deadly at times, which can attack us through the skin. There are 10 times more bacteria than human cells in our body and at such an early stage our immunological system has not yet fully developed. So, our little bodies cannot yet defend themselves against these infections.

But our mother surprisingly defends us from the infections through her milk. With our mother's contact against our body, she absorbs the same germs that attack us and her immunological system creates the antibodies, which are transmitted to us through her milk. Until our own immunological system develops, she will keep us safe. In the meantime, we start to discover our world.

As we begin to be exposed to our surroundings, close to the first month, we begin to perceive how loud this brilliant world is and how many smells it has. This is how our senses begin to work at a maximum capacity. Inside the nose, where our sense of smell resides, we find some specialized nerves that detect chemical components in the air that we breathe and send an electrical signal to the brain, which interprets the signal as smells. These nerves are super sensitive and each smell is a new sensation.

Something similar occurs with our ears, where we find our auditory sense. In this world full of strange sounds, sound waves make the eardrum vibrate and on the other side of the eardrum, tiny bones called ossicles vibrate at the same frequency. These are the smallest bones in the body, but without them we could not hear, for they are the ones that amplify the vibrations. The amplified vibration enters into the middle ear, which aligns with a kind of delicate hair.

When the vibration passes through, the hairs vibrate also. On the bottom part, there are some fragile hairs for high frequency sounds, while on the top part are the hairs for low frequency, each one of which are 200 times thinner than the hairs on our head. With time, loud noises can damage these hairs producing a premature deterioration of our auditory system. Even though, our auditory system diminishes with age.

As for our vision, the issue is different, for we are born with our eyes underdeveloped. Even a month after birth, our vision is blurry and the majority of the world we see is black and white due to the fact that our vision, at such an early stage, is very rudimentary. The eye muscles are immature preventing our ability to keep our eyes focused. Inside the eye, the muscles from the ocular lens cannot yet focus and the lens flips the image it receives. Throughout our lives, we see the world upside down or backwards. The image reorients in our brain.

The image is formed in the retina, behind the screen on the back part of the eye. Some specialized cells in the retina transform the light it perceives into electrical signals. They also detect color information, but due to the fact that they are yet not very developed, we perceive the majority of things in black and white during our first months.

From the retina, the signals travel through the thick nerves under the brain. At the bottom is where we process visual information. When the images come, the real challenge begins, for our immature brain has not yet learned how to interpret the information. But at two months, that has changed and we can distinguish colors and forms. At four months we can identify the face of our mother and, after 7 months, we have 20/20 vision. With the arrival of our perfect vision, our physical growth also initiates and we start to gain weight an equivalent of a quarter of our corporal weight each month, but after three months that measurement diminishes.

Thus, we continue through the world until we enter puberty. In this new stage of our life, like metamorphosis, our hormones initiate us into a major transformation as we pass from being a child into being an adult and our bodies are sculpted in a very attractive way indicating the arrival of this reproductive stage. At 20 years old, the human body has managed to grow four times since birth and becomes some 21 times heavier. At 21 years old we have already left puberty and we enter into a new phase of our life; adulthood, in which generally, we feel better than at any other age in our lives.

2.2 Our Brain

As we continue growing, our brain matures. After two years we survive infancy and the majority of children can already stand up and walk on their own. Later, we begin to speak, which takes a lot of energy from the brain. It is worth mentioning that some other children manage to walk and talk a little after 7 months.

A two-year-old child can learn 10 new words per day. The area of the side of the brain used to produce language and comprehension is called the Broca. Language is what differentiates us from other animals. As adults, we can interchange complex thoughts and ideas and we teach our children not only by showing them but also by speaking to them.

At around 5 years of age, as our brain develops, we achieve another characteristic only in humans; we become aware of our own identity and our individuality. We acquire the ability to think for ourselves and we form memories that will last all our lives, like our first day of school.

During childhood, the principal task of the brain is to quickly learn and grow. Our rapid growth permits the brain to more easily make connections. This ability diminishes with age. Later, during puberty, the hypothalamus, the region that controls the temperature of our body, secretes in the brain a protein called kisspeptin, which triggers the launching of another hormone in a chain reaction throughout the entire body. These hormones have dramatically prolonged emotional and physical effects. Children experience rapid growth rates and their bodies transform. The girls become women, and the boys become men.

The brain is the most important organ in the human body. It is a mass of 100 thousand millions of nervous cells called neurons capable of generating sufficient energy, which according to the "National Geographic Channel™" can keep a light bulb lit for one day. The neurons communicate using electrical impulses and each impulse is a small fragment of thought or memory. When we hear a new word, our ears convert the sound into an electrical impulse in our brain.

New neural connections are constantly forming. Among the neurons, we find a very small opening called synapse. These openings are filled with chemical substances forming a kind of bridge by which the impulses can continue their voyage. The new connection forms a pattern, which constitutes a new memory. We learn by making new connections between the neurons and later we reinforce them with repetition. The stronger the repetition is, the longer the memory will last.

Neurons are specialized nerve cells in the reception and transmission of information. The neuron is basically the only type of connection of the nervous system and its principal function is the conduction of nervous impulses. Each one of these neurons is connected to hundreds and even thousands of other neurons forming extremely complex networks. Our memory, our speech, learning new abilities, thought, conscious movement and every function of our mind, depend on these connections. These connections develop and modify throughout life according to the learning and the experiences of the person.

Apart from connecting amongst each other, neurons also establish connections with muscles and glands to send information in the form of electrical chemical impulses. The information normally travels in the form of electrical impulses through the neurons and when the impulses reach the end, they release a substance known as neurotransmitter that crosses the little space between the neurons to finally make contact with the specialized receptors located in the other cell to activate or deactivate it.

The brain consists of the brain stem, the cerebellum and the cerebrum. The brain stem is the part that controls the reflexes and the automatic functions of our body like blood pressure, heart rhythm and digestion.

The cerebellum is located in the inferior part of the brain and directly on top of the brain stem. The brain utilizes information it receives from the brain stem and the motor cortex to coordinate our movements. The cerebellum can also detect the position of our arms, hands and legs, which allows us to maintain our posture and balance. All our voluntary movements, from moving our fingers, moving our legs to walk, etc. depend on the cerebellum.

The Cerebrum is where almost all the high level functions, such as abstract thinking take place. In human beings, the cerebrum makes up about 85 percent of the weight of the brain. It is divided into two hemispheres that subdivide into a series of lobes. A band composed of about 200-250 million neurons called corpus callosum connects both hemispheres, the right and the left. The right part of the brain controls the left side of the body and the left part of the brain controls the right side of the body.

The right hemisphere is the dominant one as far as special abilities like recognizing faces, visual images, and music. The left side is dominant as far as mathematical abilities, logic, and computation. This is not a blunt division of course, since both hemispheres connect and communicate with each other. Our brain weighs about three pounds and consumes around 20 percent of the body's energy.

2.3 The Processes of Renewal and Aging

There are two key processes in the life of each one of our cells. One of them is the process of renewal through which our cells are regenerating themselves constantly. So even if I am 60 years old, the oldest organ in my body will not be more than 11 years old. The other process is the one I did not want to mention, for besides not liking it, it is the one that never fails, it is the process of aging.

The trillion of cells that form our organs and tissues, with time wear out or become damaged. But our incredible organism forms new cells, which grow and divide to replace the old ones, which is known as the **process of renewal**. In this process, some tissues regenerate with more speed, like our hair and nails.

Hair is made up of modified dead skin cells. Each strand of hair grows from a follicle encrusted in the skin. The modified cell grows here and later dies when a new cell pushes it up. This column of dead cell is what we called hair. A person can grow up to more than 15 centimeters of hair per year. Under normal conditions, hair will always continue to grow whether we want it to or not.

It is very important in this process of renewal of the organism to provide our body proper maintenance with a decent diet and appropriate exercise. This way, we tone our heart and lungs so they can work more efficiently and strengthen our bones to stimulate the bone cells in the renewal of the bone fibers. Specialized cells eat the old or damaged bone while other cells reconstruct them with a newer material more resistant. As a result, we will have denser and stronger bones. Likewise, the 650 muscles that form our body grow and fortify.

During the process of renewal, our body completely replaces organs every 11 years. The question would then be; why do we age? During the stage of aging, the process of renewal or mechanism of the organism to remain rejuvenated begins to decay and the copies that are being made of the cells to replace the old ones are not 100% the same, since the mechanism of copying them has also suffered wear, like it occurs with any printer that we have in our home or at the office.

After the vitality of our bodies during our 20s, we enter into a new stage as the **process of aging** begins. During this stage our aging accelerates, since the mechanism our body uses to prevent it, has also started to age. Our physical changes become more noticeable after our 40s. At 45, the accumulated effects of all these years, during which we have exposed our body to the sun, produce the first symptoms of aging, wrinkles.

Since our birth, our body replaces skin cells at an incredibly fast rate. We can produce up to 30 thousand new cells each minute to replace the cells we constantly shed. At 45 years of age, we have shed more than 200 kilos of dead skin cells. But, regardless of the age, the cells of our skin are never older than a few months. Skin cells remain in good condition thanks to collagen. However, ultra violet radiation in sunlight triggers a chain reaction that degrades the collagen thinning the fiber till it breaks. Therefore our skin loses its elasticity and we get wrinkles.

Our vision also changes and we start wearing glasses to read. The problem with vision is in the lens of the eye due to the cells in the internal lens, which along with the hard cells, and like the majority of brain cells, are the only cells that our body never replaces. These lens cells of the eyes are the same ones we had as children. As our ocular lens ages, it becomes more rigid and no longer focuses as well as before and our eyes begin to dry, since we produce less fluid to lubricate them and less tears to wash them.

With middle age, our body shape also changes and in this stage not even exercise is sufficient to keep us in form. When we were adolescents we could eat anything we wanted to. Now our metabolism is changing and we gain weight easier. The explanation is in our blood. At middle age, the levels of various hormones begin to lower, like estrogen, testosterone, and the growth hormones, and we begin to lose the leanness in our muscles.

We lose almost 7 pounds of muscle every 10 years of our adult age. Less muscle means that our bodies burn fewer calories, and if we continue eating at the same pace as always, the excess of food converts into fat. But the fat is not the only health risk that we run at this age. Stress also plays an important role in our deterioration. Middle age is very stressful and stress wears us out, but the damage does not end here. Stress accelerates the process of aging in our bodies.

At 50, our body slows down, but it seems like our way of life doesn't. Having a growing family and a demanding profession, also impact the process of aging since this adds more stress to our lives. This stress manifests itself in sweaty hands, loss of breath, and dizziness, but the real damage takes place inside our body. Our bodies adopt a fight or flight mode in response to stressful situations. Hormones, adrenaline, and cortisone flow from our adrenal gland to our bloodstream. Our muscles and arteries contract, the heart pumps faster and our blood pressure shoots up. We evolved the instinct of fight or flight in order to rapidly respond to the attack of a predator, but to have this instinct constantly activated causes certain damage to our cardiovascular system.

Stress accelerates the aging of our blood vessels. High blood pressure damages the cells of the walls of the arteries, which become more rigid and thicker especially the most important artery, the Aorta. The arteries with more rigid and thicker walls restrict the flow of blood. As the pressure of blood increases, our heart is forced to work harder.

It is a vicious cycle, the more stress the more damage to our blood vessels, and the more damage to the blood vessels the less chances we have to deal with stress. If the problem becomes constant or out of control, and the heart expands while fighting to pump blood to our already reduced and less elastic blood vessels, the high pressure of the blood can cause the vessels to rupture in the brain, which is known as a cerebral vascular accident or CVA.

The majority of the people learn to handle stress. However, for women in their 50s, another factor that worsens the problem is; menopause. At this age, the woman's ovaries stop releasing eggs and also stop producing the sex hormones; estrogen and progesterone, which show signs of the end of the reproductive life of the woman.

When the supplies of these hormones are reduced, the regions of the brain that control the mood, sleep and body temperature are destabilized. When the hypothalamus is out of control, a rise in temperature or hot flashes occurs. At those moments it seems like your bodies cannot set the thermostat correctly. The bones and muscle tissues debilitate. The woman's body spends all the time getting used to her hormones and now they are no longer there. Imagine how our dear women feel.

The aging process continues its accelerated path. At 60 years of age, our children have already left and we no longer work and we enter another phase in life, old age. At 70, we are in the final stretch of our walk through life, where we retire and our lives slow down and the signs of aging accelerate. The tissues of our lungs have thickened making the alveoli in our lungs less elastic, which lessens our air intake with every breath. Besides this, at this age, our brain has reduced 10%, which explains why we feel confused and forgetful.

Old age also attacks our senses. We slowly lose our auditory sense. The high frequency hairs inside our ear practically no longer exist and we are even losing hairs in the lower frequency zone. During these years, we struggle to hear. Not only hearing is difficult, seeing is also challenging. The ocular lens is more rigid and has changed its yellowish brown color due to the exposure to ultraviolet light throughout our life. The sun also causes crystals to form in the lens and our brain has to work harder to compensate for it. The process of aging accelerates at 40 and 70, due to the mechanism in the process of renewal that has worn out with age.

Another important factor is oxygen. We need it to live but slowly throughout our life it poisons us. Inside each of our cells, exist organelles called mitochondria, which are like small energy plants that combine food with oxygen. The mitochondria create the energy we need, but just like energy plants, they also generate contamination. In this case, the contaminating agent is oxygen. The mitochondria change the oxygen molecules into unstable forms called free radicals. During our lives, these free radicals suffocate the mitochondria and damage our cells.

Our cells and our DNA damage themselves more and more and the repair system fails. The imperfections accumulate and our organs eventually fail. DNA is what makes us who we are, how we will develop, and also determines how long we will live. We live until our cells can no longer be copied. Death is like life; it is a biological process. It is believed that before dying, our bloodstream is inundated with endorphins, the annihilator of the body pain, so that our tissue, in the absence of oxygen, can function, but within 10 seconds the electrical activity of the brain falls. Hearing is the last sense to cease. It can take up to 24 hours for our skin cells to stop dividing and about 37 hours for our last living cell in the brain to release its final impulse.

This fascinating story of our incredible human body, in the style of "Discovery Science Channel™" and the "National Geographic Channel™", shows us the internal and wonderful world that our organism travels through from our conception, passing through all the stages of life, to achieve our objective of living and later death. Knowing the facets through which our body goes through, apart from being interesting, also helps us to understand it better with the purpose of providing it all the care and maintenance necessary for its good performance so that in this way it can help us achieve a full life.

2.4 Physical Health

In order for our bodies to accompany us in our walk through the paths of life in search of our happiness, we must provide it with care and necessary maintenance. To have good physical health, it is necessary to understand the period of maintenance our body passes through each day of our existence, as well as, understand the formation of our eating habits throughout the years. Of course, a balanced diet is also key factor in maintaining our bodies physically healthy and not overweight. Finally, exercise tones and gives shape to our body in order to lead us through the path of good living.

The Period of Maintenance

The good health of our body begins with the understanding of the period of maintenance and its importance in preserving our body in its best shape. During this period of maintenance, a process of monitoring by our subconscious mind takes place in our organism, in search of any type of threat that affects its proper function. Later, a process of detoxification takes place and then, the process of renewal of the organism cells.

This maintenance takes place every day while our body sleeps. After we fall asleep and we find ourselves in complete darkness, our subconscious mind gives instructions to the organism to initiate the cycle of maintenance, which generally starts close to midnight and ends a little before 7 in the morning. During this lapse of time, after checking that the organism is functioning normal, it proceeds in its detoxification of what has been eaten or drunk during the day. Later, it begins the process of generating new cells to replace the old ones. By the time we wake up, our body should be completely restored.

It is of extreme importance to sleep well and for at least 7 hours to maintain a healthy body and for this it is important that the period of maintenance takes place every day and with the least possible interruption of the daily cycle. Having to wake up soon after having fallen asleep, whether because of pain, or any other health problem, or for any worry, perturbs the initiation of the cycle. Also, excess of food or drinking mainly before bed time have a negative impact in the process of detoxification, since the body will have to dedicate additional time to detoxify, which will be deducted from the time it normally takes the organism to process the renewal.

If a person falls asleep after midnight, his period of maintenance will be shortened and perhaps will not be sufficient to complete the cycle with success. If besides going to bed late, the person goes to bed drunk, the short period of maintenance will probably not be sufficient to finish detoxifying his body, which would in turn not allow the process of renewal to initiate. By not giving our body the opportunity to renew its cells daily, we are accelerating its aging.

We should instead try to go to bed daily before midnight and sleep about 7 hours, avoid heavy foods and eat lightly, preferably fruits if possible, as my good friend Alex does, to help the period of maintenance to reduce the time of detoxification and thus have more time available for the renewal of the cells. Besides the maintenance period, it is necessary to also understand why we eat the way we do it and at the times we do it. In other words, we need to understand our eating habits.

Our Eating Habits

Nowadays, when we speak about our body health or physical health it is to speak about food and exercise. For our ancestors, their nourishment was always accompanied by exercise throughout their whole life since men and women left Africa some 3.7 million years ago to populate the world. During that time, we had to walk very far to find food.

In the beginning, we ate everything we could, as long as we had something to eat. First, because we had not yet developed methods to conserve our food, and second, because we did not know when would be the next time we would eat. This was perfectly logical.

What does not make sense is that today in our modern era, where we have all types of technology to preserve our food and know exactly at what time to eat each day, we continue eating with more desperation than our ancestors. Definitely, we have inherited our eating habits from them, which is not a problem; we must simply make the necessary adjustments to eat only the amount of food necessary according to our activity and most important according to our age.

We see middle-aged people eating like adolescents. It is perfectly justifiable for an adolescent to eat everything he sees on the table, for he is still in a stage where he needs that amount of food to continue growing. But after we stop growing, why eating so much? In this stage, since we do not need so much food the body is forced to convert it into fat. That is why we always see those extra pounds at middle age. This is even more so, if we have submerged ourselves into a sedentary life.

Now, the problem is not being over weighted, but with that begins all aches and pains of middle age like high blood pressure, aches in the muscles, bones, and joints. These in turn, generate other types of problems which, depending on the attitude we have developed by then, could lessen our physical health. This is why we should have a very balanced diet.

A Balanced Diet

Unlike our ancestors, today we can have any diet we want. However, the recommendation would be to have a balanced diet with all the nutritional components. Except, we have some medical justification to modify it. A balanced diet is one, which through the nourishment that makes up part of each meal, provides nutrients in proportions that the healthy organism needs for its good performance.

Consuming large amounts of food can cause disorders in the digestive system. Besides, eating in excess can cause overweight and obesity, which can increase the risk of hypertension, heart problems, diabetes and arthritis. We should also not consume so much saturated fat and sugar, since these elevate the risk of having cardiovascular diseases.

When our body processes the ingredients in our food (with the exception of indigestible fibers), it obtains its energy. This energy is commonly measured in calories. These calories are necessary for each part of the body to fulfill its functions. From the food processing vitamins and minerals are also obtained so that such process of getting energy from food can adequately take place. The food components are grouped into two types; the micronutrients and the macronutrients.

Micronutrients are made up of vitamins and minerals. These components are necessary in lesser quantities and that is why they are known as micronutrients. The macronutrients create the appropriate means by which micronutrients can do their job. This indicates to us that the vitamins and minerals we take are useless, if we don't eat the necessary foods that optimize the conditions for their use.

Macronutrients are the principal nutrients that make up the food we eat in our daily diet. Among these macronutrients we have: carbohydrates, proteins, and fats. The macronutrients are the ones that provide the energy to the organism. Under normal conditions, our diet should include approximately 50% of carbohydrates, 25% of proteins, and 25% of fats.

Carbohydrate Portion
Half of the calories of our organism are obtained from the carbohydrates contained in foods like fruits, vegetable, cereals, grains, bread, rice, pasta, etc. Carbohydrates or hydrates of carbon, also called sugars, are the most abundant and diverse organic compounds. They are formed by carbon, hydrogen and oxygen, which is how they got their name. Carbohydrates are classified as simple and complex. Simple carbohydrates are rapidly absorbed sugars and generate an immediate secretion of insulin, a hormone produced by the beta cells inside the pancreas. With each food, the beta cells release inulin to help the organism use or store the blood glucose they obtain from the food.

Simple carbohydrates are found in refined sugars, honey, marmalade, syrups, sweets, milk, vegetables, and fruits. They provide calories but little nutritional value. Besides, they contribute to gaining weight easily, which is why the consumption of them should be moderate. Complex carbohydrates are those that are absorbed slower, and act more like stored energy. Among these carbohydrates are: cereals, legumes, bread, pastas, rice and grains.

The principal function of carbohydrates is to provide energy to the body in order to fulfill all its vital activities. Our metabolism transforms them into glucose, which passes into the bloodstream and is consumed by all the cells of the body. There is a part of carbohydrates, which is transformed into fat, which is accumulated in the organism. Carbohydrates provide four kilocalories for each gram consumed.

In a diet of 1,500 kilocalories a day, one should consume 750 kilocalories or 187 grams of carbohydrates, assuming that half of the diet is carbohydrates. Fruits and vegetables would be preferable. It is important to vary your food and to know how to combine it. The excess of carbohydrates in our diet can produce obesity. However, the lack of carbohydrates can cause bad nutrition.

Protein Portion
One fourth of our calories are obtained through proteins, which are the nutrients necessary for our organism to repair and construct its structures. We obtain proteins from foods of animal origin like: red meats, fish, fowl, eggs, and dairy products. We can also obtain these foods from vegetable origin like: dried fruits, soy, legumes, mushrooms, and cereals. Foods of animal origin contain diverse types of fat, whose excess can cause damage to our health. It is recommended to eat lean meat, or meat free of fat.

The number of calories that are obtained from these foods should be sufficient to provide at least one gram of protein for every kilogram of the lean weight of your body, which is the weight of your muscles, organs, bones, and skin without including water or the fat which is housed in the tissues.

Lean weight is approximately 70% of the total weight of the body. For example, if a person weighs 75 kilos, his lean weight is 52 kilos, in other words, 70% of 75. If for each one of those 52 kilos, the person has to eat one gram of lean protein each day, his daily intake of protein would be 52 grams to maintain his weight.

It is important to stress those proteins like milk and its derivatives, chicken, eggs, fish, and red meat increase cholesterol, which is why skim milk, low fat dairy products, as well as lean meats are recommended. Fats and sugar should be very limited even if we are skinny and in normal condition.

Fat Portion
The other one fourth of our calories comes from fats, which are a good source of energy, producing more than twice the energy of the organism. Fats are stored in the body to be utilized later, in case there is a reduction in carbohydrates. Fat, apart from being the body's reserved energy storage, also protects us against cold and facilitates the absorption and mobility in the bloodstream of oil based vitamins like A, D, E, and K. However, the excessive consumption of fats can produce obesity, heart disease, and some types of cancer.

Fats are divided into two types: saturated fats and unsaturated fats. The type of fat in the diet, as well as the total quantity that is consumed, is important in relation to health. Saturated fats are considered harmful for the health and differentiate from the other fats for being the ones that remain solid at room temperature and only become liquids if they are heated. They are mainly found in animal products like meats and it derivatives: lactates like milk, cheese, cream etc., although, they can also be found, but in lesser quantities, in vegetable products like coconut oil, palm oil, and peanut oil.

Saturated fats tend to increment the concentration of cholesterol in the blood, which is why they are not desirable, since they contribute to the development of arteriosclerosis and heart disease. Cholesterol is found in saturated fats of animal origin. To avoid the damage they can produce to your health, their consumption should be reduced.

Unsaturated fats are healthier. We find them in vegetable oils like olive oil; in fish like salmon, tuna, sardines, etc., in seeds, nuts, and hazelnuts. The consumption of unsaturated fats can be beneficial to the organism.

Besides the intake of carbohydrates, proteins and a portion of fat, it is recommended to drink at least 7 glasses of water daily to eliminate the toxins in the body. Alcohol, caffeine, and sugar, should be avoided, especially if one is stressed. Caffeine contained in tea, coffee, drinks with cola, etc., can give us a sensation of more energy, but could also increase stress and affect the nervous system.

Of course, diets are a matter of taste. Some prefer to eat what they like as opposed to what is more nutritious for them. This would not be a problem if it were compensated with complete vitamins and minerals necessary to maintain our bodies in shape and avoid becoming overweight.

Overweight

Overweight is defined as the abnormal or excessive accumulation of fat, which is harmful to our health. By taking in more calories than the organism can burn, the body accumulates leftover calories in the form of fat. Perhaps doing this from time to time would not affect us too much, since a little bit of body fat does not become a health risk in the majority of people. But, when a person habitually eats more calories than necessary, then the extra-accumulated fat can become a serious problem since it could cause some complications to develop. In fact, the majority of health problems in adults start with weight gain.

Overweight is determined by the calculation of the body mass index or BMI, which is an indicator of the relationship between the weight and the height of the person. To obtain the BMI, the body weight in pounds is divided into the height of the person in inches squared, then multiplied by a conversion factor of 703. For example, if a person weighs 165 pound and measures 65.74 inches in height, his body mass index is 27. This means that this person is overweight. Any person who has a BMI greater than 25 is considered overweight and when it passes 30, that person is considered obese. As we can see, being overweight is the first step towards obesity. This is why we should try to avoid it or at least control it. The ideal weight of a person is that one that produces a BMI of 18-25.

Normally, overweight in a person is the result of eating more than the organism needs. In an obese person, being overweight is related to some illness like hypothyroidism. Currently, obesity is considered an increasing public health problem worldwide. Today there are more overweight people than in the past; in fact, there are more young people that are developing health problems like hypertension, high cholesterol and type 2 diabetes. These health problems used to only affect adults.

Various factors exist which contribute to the actual cause of being overweight. One of those factors is genetics; since genes contribute in determining the ways each person stores and burns fat. Besides, genes as well as eating habits are transmitted from parents to children, which make it possible for various members of the same family to have overweight problems. Another influencing factor is a person's lifestyle. Eating healthy food, exercising and living a non-sedentary life helps us avoid those extra pounds. At times, excessive weight gain is due to endocrine problems, genetic syndromes or even medications. Being overweight is not only an esthetic problem; it is also a health problem that should be taken care of promptly.

Being overweight can cause health problems like diabetes and cardiac diseases. It can also affect joints, breathing, sleep, moods and energy levels. In other words, it can have negative repercussions in the quality of life of a person. This is why we should start doing something to avoid it, like limiting our consumption of fats, increasing our consumption of fruits, vegetables, legumes, cereals, dried fruits, limiting sugars, doing exercise, and maintaining a normal weight.

Exercise

Physical exercise is essential to remain healthy, counter attack the effects of a sedentary life, and diminish stress. By moving around, our blood transports more oxygen to the muscles increasing their capacity to do work. Exercises help us maintain our body in shape revealing muscle tone and definition. However, exercise is of much more importance during our youth, before our adult life. During this stage, exercising will have a tremendously positive influence on our body for the rest of our lives, by helping us maintain our cells and organs in good condition.

Exercise fortifies the heart, which is the muscle that works the most in our body without taking any rest, not even for 27 seconds, till the end of life. Also, exercise makes the muscles in the heart more efficient. Each contraction will pump more blood so the heart can beat slower and thus prolong life.

Exercises also make changes in the lungs, which grow extra capillaries to absorb more oxygen with each breath. We also breathe more deeply causing each alveolus in the lungs to fill completely. Exercise also strengthens our skeleton, since the bones absorb pressure, which stimulates the cells in the bones to renew their fibers and strengthen them.

Other benefits from exercises are: reduction in overweight, decrease in cholesterol and risk of heart attack, production of endorphins which help us relax, enhance our mood, and distraction from our worries. They can even help us eliminate the intake of any toxin in our foods.

2.5 Vitamins and Minerals

We have heard that education is the most important tool for the development of human beings, for, as individuals develop, countries develop, too. However, for us to develop, we need to learn the knowledge taught to us in education and for this, we must have adequate nutrition, to which vitamins and minerals are essential. This is why it is very important to know what vitamins and minerals are, the processes of oxidation and reduction, free radicals, and the importance of vitamins in our lives. In fact, our happiness is tied to vitamins, especially B complex vitamins.

Vitamins

Vitamins are groups of organic compounds constituted by chains of carbon, hydrogen and oxygen in different arrangements. Sometimes they are made up of sulfur, phosphorous, and other chemical elements. Vitamins are necessary for life and their deficiencies can cause illnesses. Other compounds or substances exist which produce certain benefits when we take them, but a deficiency in them does not cause any illness at all. These compounds are called nutrients and cannot be considered vitamins.

In the beginning, as different types of vitamins were discovered, they were named with letters of the alphabet. We have: vitamins A, B, C, D, E, etc. Past investigations have proven that vitamin B has multiple components with specific capabilities to prevent certain illnesses. Therefore, they were called B complex and it was decided to assign a sub number to the letter B. Therefore, we have: B1, B2, B3, B6, and B12. Vitamins B4, B5, B7, B8, B9, B10 and B11 resulted being part of the other B vitamins. For this reason, they were removed from the list. Lately, investigators have tried to call vitamins by their chemical compound name. For example: Thiamine for B1, Niacin for B2, Ascorbic Acid for vitamin C, etc. Vitamins can be oil based, which can dissolve in oil like A and E. They can also be water based which dissolve in water like B and C.

The purpose of vitamins is to help convert foods into energy. Normally they are utilized in the interior of cells, where thousands of enzymes are made, which regulate the necessary chemical reactions for the well-functioning of the cells. So, the required energy to blink, move a finger, breathe; as well as, the signals from the brain that make the heartbeat, that make you sense and respond to the need to breath, eat, sleep, or dream, depend on these chemical reactions perfectly orchestrated by the cells in the body. Each one of these chemical reaction depend on substances call enzymes to accelerate or catalyze the reaction. Each one of these enzymes needs at the same time other substances call coenzymes essential for its activity. These coenzymes are normally vitamins or minerals or both.

In other words, our organism cannot function without vitamins and minerals. These chemical reactions, accelerated by enzymes and vitamins and minerals, normally participate in the movement or transferring around of the different chemical structures, transforming one type of molecule into another, or in the aggregation or disaggregation of hydrogen atoms between molecules, which gives origin to the processes of oxidation and reduction.

Processes of Oxidation and Reduction

Our body is an infinite collection of atoms and molecules. Each organ, each tissue, each protein, enzyme, or cell is formed by these atoms and molecules. The atoms exist in a neutral electric state with their electrons circling around the nucleus of the atom. The electrons are negatively charged particles, while the nucleus or central part is positively charged. Normally, the negative charges equal the positive charges, which form electrically balanced atoms or neutrons. However, if everything remained electrically neutral, we would not be able to survive, since the functioning of our bodies depends on the generation of energy through the flirtation of these electrons from one molecule to the other in a controlled manner.

The activity of generating the energy required by the body to fulfill all its functions occurs in each cell, mainly inside the internal structures of the cell called mitochondria, our energy factory. In the generation of energy, when a molecule wins or accepts an electron, the process is called *reduction*. Now, when a molecule loses or gives another an electron, then the process is called *oxidation*. By losing or giving up and electron, the balanced number of electrons around the nucleus is broken converting the molecule in what is known as a free radical.

Free Radicals

Free radicals are formed when molecules oxidize or lose an electron. By trying to equip their number of electrons, free radicals become very reactive, which can on one side, generate much energy, but on the other side, can damage other molecules. In the process of stealing an electron from another molecule to reestablish its electrical balance, a molecule can damage, alter, or age another molecule.

Normally, free radicals do their dirty job against the DNA, which forms the essential genetic material in the nucleus of each cell, and stores all the information that makes us function. Any damage to this genetic material can make the cells dangerous converting them into cancerous seeds. We see then, that free radicals can be necessary for your health, but they can also be harmful. As long as the formation of free radicals is controlled, everything is fine. But unfortunately, this is not always the case.

The effects of solar light, the ozone, smoking, and food additives that we eat and the oxygen in the air that we breathe, contribute to the formations of these free radicals that accelerate the process of aging and the development of illnesses. The proper functioning of the immune system of the body depends on the impact with which these free radicals are released by the white blood cells in their defensive assault against the viruses and bacteria to protect us from infections.

In regards to oxygen, the body utilizes it like a source of energy and life. By burning them, free radicals remain as residue, which affect and wear out our organism. These free radicals are the cause of a great deal of illnesses. Stress, contamination, medications, etc., increase the quantity of free radicals in our body. The way to combat them is through the antioxidants contained in some foods, or directly through vitamins and minerals. In this sense, we have as an example, Vitamin C, apart from its antioxidant effects; it fortifies our immune system, which weakens under stress.

On the other hand, the lack of magnesium, potassium, and calcium, prevents the body from reducing the damage provoked by the hormones generated by stress. Besides, these minerals are relaxers and help us maintain a stable cardiac rhythm. Therefore, to combat the damages of stress and to maintain us healthy, in general, a mixed and balanced diet that provides us these minerals is important.

Therefore, what we can do to protect ourselves or to at least minimize the harmful effects of these free radicals is definitely to take our vitamins and minerals in the correct types and doses. Due to the fact that the damage from free radicals basically comes from the process of oxidation, the group of vitamins and minerals used to contain this damage has been called *antioxidants*. Among the vitamins that fall under this group of antioxidants are: vitamins A, C, and E. Among the minerals that fall under this group of antioxidants we have: selenium and zinc. Antioxidants have proven, in different studies, to be very effective in reducing aging, preventing heart attacks, and reducing cases of cancer.

The Importance of Vitamins

Since the first case of beriberi; an illness caused by the deficiency of vitamin B1 which affects the nervous, muscular and digestive systems; around the year 2,500 B.C., up to the illness of scurvy; caused by a deficiency in vitamin C which began with weariness, fatigue and irritability, followed by bleeding and inflammation of the gums; that destroyed a large amount of people in those olden times, the deficiency in vitamins have played an important role.

The discovery of the relationship between illnesses and the deficiency of vitamins, originated the concept of dietary deficiency as a result of the illnesses at the end of the XIX century. In the following century, it is discovered that some foods contained chemical compounds called amines that contained nitrogen and that prevented certain illnesses. This discovery was called: *vitamin*, from the Latin vita for life and the chemical compound amine.

It is the deficiency of vitamins what produces illnesses. It is perhaps that deficiency that we inherit from our parents and not the illnesses itself. But the problem is not the deficiency but to know if we have it. A vitamin profile should be done on a child at birth to determine what he lacks and design a proper diet that will permit him to overcome those deficiencies. Also, vitamins are important when we are continually stressed, since our body resents, weakens, and our defenses get down. This is why it is essential to have a balanced diet that provides us all the necessary nutrients to help us with stress and to keep us healthy.

There are also some vitamins and minerals to which we should owe special attention to. The vitamin "B" complex, in my opinion, is responsible for the happiness of a person. The lack of this vitamin complex, apart from debilitating our nervous system, makes us feel unhappy and with a tendency to think negatively. Some other vitamins like A, C, and E provide us with the antioxidants necessary to combat free radicals.

Minerals

Minerals, like vitamins, have as a basic function to act as cofactors to help accelerate the thousands of millions of chemical reactions that occur all the time in our bodies. Minerals form part of the bone and dental structure, regulate the balance of water inside and outside a cell, and intervene in neural and muscular activity. Minerals are inorganic elements that play a critical role in the well-functioning of the body, in which they represent almost four percent of our body weight and distribute themselves proportionally in all the tissues.

Among the most important minerals in our body are calcium, phosphorous, sodium, potassium, iodine, and zinc. It is required to obtain all the minerals we need from the food we eat, since not one of them is produced by the body. Some of these minerals, the ones called macro-minerals, are needed in higher doses like calcium, phosphorous, sodium, chlorine, potassium and magnesium. The other ones called micro-minerals like iron, zinc, iodine, etc., are needed in smaller doses.

Apart from their basic function, minerals also have other functions. For example, *calcium,* which is the most abundant mineral in our bodies, provides strength and hardness to bones and teeth, and stimulates muscle contraction. Ninety nine percent of the calcium in our body is in our bones. We obtain this mineral by eating dairy products like milk, yogurt, curd, cheeses, etc. A lack in this mineral can produce problems in children's growth, or can cause rickets, osteoporosis, or loss of bone density, osteomalacia, or the softening of bones associated with the lack of vitamin D. It can also cause convulsions. On the other hand, an excess of calcium can generate calcifications.

Phosphorous is the second most abundant mineral in the organism with 80% of it concentrated in our bone. Like calcium, phosphorous also provides strength and hardness to bones and teeth and is necessary to appropriately metabolize proteins, fat and carbohydrates. It also acts like a cofactor in many chemical reactions in the body and regulates the use of B complex.

Phosphorous is obtained by eating meats, fish, eggs, dairy, dried fruits, cereals and legumes. A lack of this mineral can produce weakness and demineralization to the bone.

Iron is found predominantly 75% in the hemoglobin of the blood that transports oxygen to our cells. It is necessary for the utilization of vitamins in the B complex, collaborates in the immune system and intervenes in the function and synthesis of neurotransmitters. The principal sources of iron are meats and fish, legumes, dried fruits, and leafy vegetables. A lack of this mineral can produce anemia, weakness, and a greater risk of infections.

Magnesium, together with calcium, stimulates muscular contraction and the coagulation of the blood. It also participates in the metabolism of the carbohydrates, in the transmission of nerve impulse, and in the correct functioning of the immune system. This mineral is obtained from vegetables and green legumes, fruits, dried fruits, cereals, cocoa, fish and seafood. A lack of it can produce problems in growth, alterations in behavior, weakness, and spasms.

Sodium, chlorine, and *potassium* are found distributed in the different liquids of the body. These minerals regulate water content inside and outside the cells, intervene in the transmission of nerve impulse and muscular activity. We obtain sodium and chlorine from common salt and potassium from vegetable, dried fruits, cereal and potatoes. A lack of sodium or chlorine is related to muscular cramps, mental confusion, and lack of appetite. A deficit in potassium is associated with muscular weakness and paralysis. An excess of sodium is related to an increase in arterial pressure, liquid retention, and renal overload. While an excess of chlorine is associated with vomiting, an excess of potassium is associated to muscular weakening with the risk of cardiac alterations.

Zinc is a micro-mineral that is essential for the correct functioning of the body. Eighty five percent of our reserves of this great mineral are deposited in the muscles, bones, testicles, hair, nails and pigmented tissues in the eye. Zinc participates in the functioning of the prostate gland and the development of the reproductive organs, in the synthesis of proteins and collagen, helps heal wounds, strengthens the defenses of the body, and protects the liver. It's indispensable for the correct formation of the bones, is a component of corporal insulin; is a powerful antioxidant and also maintains the sense of taste and smell in good shape. You can obtain zinc by eating meats, fish, egg yolk, fowls, sardines, and seafood, legumes, pecans, cereals, etc.

3. The Wonderful Human Mind

In the previous chapter we learned about the incredible human body in order to be and keep ourselves in good physical health. In this way, our body can heartily accompany us through our walk through life helping us achieve happiness. In this chapter, we will continue discovering our body, but this time we will concentrate on the wonderful human mind, to know how this wonder called the mind functions, formed after a long process of evolution.

In our mind originate emotions, which we should understand so we can control them and thus, make sure they do not lessen our quality of life. From the mind also come our thoughts, which make us who we are. Our thoughts have permitted us to conquer the planet; however, on the path we are headed, they could lead us to its destruction, if we do not embrace a more positive way of thinking. It is simply a matter of intelligence, as the total sum of all its parts. Our mind is key to the future of the human race, which is why we should take care of it with good mental health. A sound mind can maintain a healthy body.

3.1 Evolution of the Human Mind

Human beings should know the wonders of their mind, which is a product of a long evolutionary process. As our brain developed for millions of years, so did the human mind. Can you imagine how we would be if we had no consciousness of ourselves, or of the world that surrounds us? What if we were unable to generate a single thought, and that we move through life without purpose? To know our mind's functioning and enter into its conscious level is something fascinating, but much more fascinating is submerging into its bowels, the subconscious.

Evolution of the Brain

Throughout millions of years, our brain has been able to evolve from the primitive brain, which we inherited from fish and reptiles to the brain we have today, capable of feeling and thinking. The human brain is a mass of about 3 pounds of cells and nerve tissues almost three times as big as primates, our closest relatives in the evolutionary process.

The primitive brain, also known as the brain stem, is what surrounds the upper part of the spinal cord, from where it regulates the basic vital functions to ensure the survival of the human being, for example, its breathing and metabolism and controlling the reactions and movements of the body. With the primitive brain, we could feel, but perhaps not think. This brain was more emotional.

The most primitive sense of the emotional brain is the sense of smell, with which after analyzing the smells transported by the wind, we could detect the existence of other living species. The emotional brain could distinguish between something nutritious, like prey, something poisonous or dangerous like a predator, and even could detect a sexual partner. It better not be wrong! In those primitive times, detecting smells became the supreme sense for survival.

The ancient centers of emotion began to evolve from smell, which initially was composed by thin layers of neurons to analyze the smell. One of those layers of neurons would take the smell and classify it as food or toxin, sexual partner, friend or enemy. A second layer would send messages to the nervous system indicating to the organism to bite or not bite, get close or flee.

In the brain of the first mammals, new layers of the emotional brain evolved around the brain stem. This new portion of nerve tissues is known as the limbic system, which is composed by the thalamus, hypothalamus, hippocampus, and the amygdala.

As it evolved, the limbic system developed the ability to learn and memorize. These two powerful tools allowed an animal to be much more intelligent, to better adapt to the ever changing scenarios it encountered. For example, if a food produced a discomfort, it could be avoided the second time.

Decisions like what should be eaten and what should be discarded were still determined mainly by smell. Thanks to the interrelated work of the olfactory bulb and the limbic system, smells were distinguished and recognized in order to later compare them with past smells and determine if they were good or bad.

Throughout evolution, the brain has grown from the bottom to the top. Apart from the primitive brain, where emotional centers surged, additional layers of tissues formed later on. This new part of the brain is known as the neocortex, from which evolved the thinking brain. We can see that the emotional brain, with which we feel, existed way before the rational brain with which we think. Now, thoughts are intertwined with feelings, which is very important to know in order to better understand our emotions.

After the neocortex formed, the brain continued to evolve with time. Already, in the "Homo Sapiens" that lived 200 thousand years ago, the neocortex was much bigger than in any other species. The neocortex is the seat of the brain. It contains the centers that compare and understand what the senses perceive. Besides, it adds to a feeling what we think about it and this permits us to have feelings in respect to ideas, art, symbols, and the imagination. It is the neocortex what makes us human. In its evolution, the neocortex created mechanisms along the way that would help the person to survive when faced with adversity. In this sense, the neocortex came to be capable of designing strategies and plans on long term in order to conquer the world.

What Is This Wonder Called Mind?

The human mind can be defined as a set of faculties that the human being has to perceive, remember, consider, and evaluate information to make decisions for its functioning and survival. The human mind resides in the brain and has three important aspects that characterize its own existence: consciousness; thoughts; and the purpose in doing what it does.

Consciousness is referred to as the knowledge that a being has of himself and his environment. Everything we perceive by our senses link the human being with the exterior world, and thanks to those sensations, he can know his nature. With our senses we perceive our world and become conscious of its existence. In the same way, we acquire consciousness of our own existence. By means of our senses we see ourselves move, we feel ourselves, and we transmit sensations from our body to our brain.

That knowledge that we have of our existence and of our world, which we call consciousness, is without a doubt, a wonder of the human being. This is what truly permits us to realize who we are. Can you imagine how the world would be if we were not capable of recognizing our environment or ourselves?

Of course, the nature of one's consciousness is going to depend on how a person thinks about themselves and the world that surrounds them, what they call their reality. A human being reacts to circumstances of life based on what they adopt as their reality, which could be different from actual reality or the reality of another person. His or her reality is the one they have constructed with thoughts ingrained from infancy or with the thoughts they have formulated inside their own mind with the passing of time.

Another fundamental aspect of the mind is thinking. Today, it is impossible to conceive of the mind without its thinking. In the beginning, millions of years ago, when the brain had not yet developed the capacity of abstract thought, it could only feel and the feeling was produced purely by emotion. What caused the body to take action was the response of the brain to those feelings. But after we began to think, our thinking could influence that feeling, which is what now makes our thinking the principal cause of our reaction.

The aforementioned suggests that the purpose of what the human mind does refers to the intention of planning a course of action with previous knowledge of its objective, or to work in a certain way toward a desired and foreseen objective. The purpose is linked to the desire, which is achieved thanks to willpower. Willpower is the mental ability to do or not to do something. Willpower along with thinking conforms with the essence of mentality or mental activity.

The Function of the Mind

In the human mind, information collected by the sensory system, flows through a system of mental processes such as thinking, ideas, imagination, memories, illusions and emotions. All the information received is organized, interpreted and finally stored in the memory. The memory is the mental ability that permits us to store, retain and recover information about past events. This stored information or memories can deteriorate and even be lost if they do not receive necessary stimuli to conserve them. Depending on the duration of the retention of the recollection, the memory can be of the sensory type, short term, or long term type.

Sensory memory registers automatically the information we obtain from our senses of the external environment that manifests itself during a brief period of one to two seconds. This information can later be transferred to short-term memory or be eliminated. Short-term memory temporarily stores information up to approximately 25 seconds. While long term memory stores greater quantities of information during long periods of time, like years or even an entire lifetime. Long-term memory is our operative memory and the one we normally refer to as our memory.

The function of the human mind can be compared to that of a computer. In fact, the computer has been created in its image and resemblance. The only difference would be, not in the speed in which information is processed, but in that the computer requires the human mind for its programming, while the human mind programs itself. Of course, we only need to learn how to do this, and for that; the only thing we should do is to follow the guidelines in subchapter 5.3 on "How to Program the Subconscious Mind".

The main function of the human mind is to give instructions to the body so it can fulfill the necessary tasks it needs to operate. In a computer, the Central Processing Unit or CPU plays the role of the mind and the computer in itself would be the body. Just like in our mind, in a computer there are two levels of activity; what we see on the screen and what takes place behind it. More than 90% of the activity occurs behind the screen, where millions of operations are taking place each second. The two levels of the human mind are the conscious and the subconscious. In the conscious or rational mind, as it is also called, only

10% of mental activity is realized, the rest takes place in the subconscious or irrational mind.

The Conscious Mind

The conscious is the superficial level of the mind where voluntary mental activities are produced while we are conscious. It is the mind that permits us to be conscious of our existence and the existence of the world that surrounds us, through our senses. The chief function of the conscious mind is to rationalize, even though it also permits us to think logically, plan, judge, and analyze.

The conscious mind is responsible for the rational thinking utilized in processing information and evaluating it in order to make logical decisions. While the conscious mind performs its daily mental activity, the subconscious mind stores information obtained from the senses and its emotions.

The Subconscious Mind

The subconscious is the most profound level of the mind where an activity is produced which we are generally not conscious of and which is perceived not by the senses, but by intuition. In the subconscious mind 90% of mental activity is generated, including the basic processes so our body can function, like eating, breathing, talking, moving, and many other processes.

The subconscious also monitors our body in search of signals of failure in health and illnesses; scans the mind itself to ensure that there are no conflicts or worries; evaluates the environment where we find ourselves in to detect any danger or threat that could put our integrity at risk. It also regulates and interprets our perceptions and emotions. It is the one that guards our memory, experiences, and intelligence.

The conscious mind is the seat of reasoning, while the subconscious mind is the seat of emotions. It is possible for both levels of the mind, the one that thinks, and the one that feels, to enter into a conflict. If the person cannot control his emotions, the emotional, or irrational mind, will dominate the thinking or rational mind.

This is when we say that a person is thinking with his heart, since we always associate emotions with the heart. The tendency of the emotional mind to prevail over the rational mind has been with us throughout the process of the evolution of emotions, but as we learn how to control our emotions, that tendency has been diminishing, making us better thinkers and less emotional.

The ideal thing would be for our minds, the emotional and the rational to work together in equilibrium and harmony to obtain the best of both, in order to navigate our way through the world. However, when passions appear, the balance is inclined towards the emotional mind, which always dominates the rational mind. For this reason, it is of great importance to know and control our emotions.

3.2 Emotions

Emotions are an inextricable part of our lives. They always go with us; they influence our decisions, which have an impact on one's quality of life. For that impact to be positive, we should manage them adequately. In order to do this, we must be conscious of our emotions, know what they are, and know the different types of common emotions that exist so that we can manage them. We should also know how they form so we can control them. In this way, we can make better decisions to resolve our everyday problems and overcomes stress. Managing and controlling our emotions makes us emotionally intelligent. It also helps us have better health and achieve better relationships with other people.

What are Emotions?

Before entering into the field of emotions, it is necessary to speak a bit about feelings and how they are related to emotions. This relationship is so tight that sometimes both terms are used interchangeably. However, there exist some differences between them, which are important to know. A feeling is an emotional disposition toward something, an act, or a person, that is produced by happy or sad events that has caused an impression on the being. Feelings determine the mood of a person. They also indicate to people how to react when faced with a situation.

It is then of vital importance that our feelings be healthy or positive. A positive feeling like love helps our mood reach happiness and our lives are made more pleasant. If on the contrary, our feelings are negative, like hate, for example, our mood loses its equilibrium and we could suffer disorders and even react against something or someone to produce harm. Positive feelings always result in favorable situations, while negative ones do the opposite. With positive feelings like love we can construct what we want, while with negative ones like hate we can only destroy.

Feelings, like emotions, are tightly interrelated in such a way that one could be part of the other. Perhaps the most marked difference between both concepts is in the duration and the intensity of each one. Feelings are more lasting than emotions, while emotions can be more intense than feelings.

An emotion can be defined as the biological or psychological reaction of a person to a determined type of situation that exercises influence over their behavior or conduct. The creation of an emotion is initiated in the brain and is manifested through certain physical changes. When the body detects some dangerous or threatening situation, it immediately draws from the resources within its reach to control the situation.

Emotions give us a defined disposition to act and signal us the direction in which we should do it. This is why we can also say that an emotion is an immediate response by our bodies to some stimulus or situation it perceives. If the stimulus is favorable for survival, the emotion is positive, otherwise, the emotion would be negative. Some of the organism reactions that unleash emotions are innate. Such as: the ones that occur in the case of primary emotions. However, some other reactions are learned from observation and from the thought we have of our environment, which is what happens with secondary emotions.

Types of Emotions

There exist two types of emotions, their classification depending on their cause. We have primary emotions and secondary emotions. Apart from these two types of emotions, we also have positive and negative emotions, which are based on how useful the emotions can be in helping us survive.

Primary Emotions

Primary emotions are those that come from innate mechanisms, and are physical and mental manifestations that generally end when the stimulus that provoked them disappears. Primary emotions form part of our survival instinct and help us in adapting to our environment. Among the primary emotions we find: happiness, sadness, anger and fear.

Happiness. It is one of the basic human emotions produced by feelings of love, pleasure, satisfaction, etc. that something or someone provokes in us. Happiness generates a general wellbeing that gives energy and a powerful disposition of doing things with enthusiasm and is expressed in the countenance, language and the general behavior of a person. We feel happiness when we obtain what we desire: success, money, love, a job, recognition, etc. and as a result of happiness, we smile and laugh.

Happiness has a great impact in our lives, for it helps us liberates our tensions, which have accumulated due to worries, anxiety, situations of stress, anguish, etc. It also favors interpersonal relationships, since it permits us be friendlier and to show the affection or the esteem we feel for someone. Happiness also reduces aggression between people.

Sadness. It is another one of the most basic and common emotions. Sadness is characterized by general feelings of discouragement, anguish, worry and loss of energy or will. Other symptoms of sadness include: listlessness, lack of appetite, etc. Under this emotion, the person feels discouragement, desire to cry, and low self-esteem. It is exactly the opposite of happiness.

This emotion is very frequently caused by mishaps in life, like illness or death of a loved one, problems with friends and family, problems at work, etc. Generally, once its cause disappears, sadness should also disappear and the person should resume his normal life. However, when the sadness is prolonged, it can turn into depression, which is an illness that needs to be treated. Besides, a prolonged sadness lasting for a long period of time can make the body ill. When my wife died, the sadness that her loss produced in her mother was prolonged for more than one year. Later, she was detected with and advanced stage of cancer.

Sadness, like any other emotion, has direct effects on us. It reduces our interest for diversion and pleasure, fixes the attention in its cause, and undercuts our energy to continue with the activities of life and leaves us in a state ready to mourn our loss, reflect over its significance, and finally, to make the psychological adjustments and new plans that would permit us to continue with our life.

One of the strategies that people use against sadness consists of simply being alone, which seems to be something attractive when we feel sad; however, frequently this only serves to add a sense of loneliness and alienation. The most popular tactic to fight against sadness is to socialize or go out with friends or family. This works well if the effect is to make the mind of the person abandon his sadness. If the person utilizes the occasion only to keep thinking on that, which made him sad, then he will simply prolong his state of sadness.

Distractions break the chain of thought, which harbor sadness. Relaxing also helps get out of it. Socializing does well, as well as, exercising, which is one of the most efficient tactics do dissipate sadness. Another resource to overcome sadness is to help other people with their problems, without being affected by them. Praying is also good for overcoming sadness.

Anger. It is the most intense of all the primary emotions, and is characterized by a high degree of neuronal discharge that can be activated by any frustration, like not being able to resolve a problem on time, or because something did not come out as expected. It can also be activated when a person feels betrayed or simply when he feels a lack of control of temperament produced by an act that occurs in a form contrary to his expectations, which in turn makes him aggressive and violent.

Anger is increased in an exponential way when the angry person tries to attack what bothers him and is contained by another person. In this stage, the anger can be very dangerous since in his quest to destroy the origin, he could be causing more unnecessary damages against himself, other people, or properties. Once the anger has passed, the negative consequences could very well leave more than just a bad taste.

Fear. It is an emotion that is experienced with the anticipations of a threat, danger, or any other situation that puts at risk our integrity and usually is accompanied with a desire to flee or fight. Fear is generated in the cerebral amygdala and when it activates, it produces a fearful sensation. Fears can be innate or acquired. The first ones are inherited, for example, by animals and by human beings. Innate fears are engraved in our genes. Among these fears are: fear of darkness; natural phenomenon like earthquakes, thunder, lightning, etc.; and fear of death.

Acquired fears come mainly from adverse experiences we have lived, or from negative beliefs that we have learned, especially during our childhood, at home, or in our environment. Given that these experiences or beliefs bring us unpleasant memories, we do not want them to be repeated, which cause us to develop fear towards certain things. To complicate things even more, these fears can become phobias like zoophobia; or fear of animals, agoraphobia; or fear of open spaces, claustrophobia; or fear of enclosed spaces, and acrophobia; or fear of heights.

Now, as far as its cause, fear can be real or imaginary. Real or rational fear obeys a real cause and is not bad. In fact, it is a mechanism of protection and self-preservation. Real fear serves as a warning sign of eminent danger or when our life is threatened. In this instance, fear then is necessary to keep us alive. If we do not feel fear in certain situations, we could fail to react in an adequate way to defend ourselves from a threat and put ourselves at great risk.

On the other hand, imaginary or irrational fear is produced by the imagination and is not good. This type of fear generally is disproportionate in relation to the threat. Imaginary fear can cause us to become paralyzed when confronted with a situation that for other people could be insignificant. This perverse fear impedes us from living our life to the fullest and being productive.

It is important then, to learn to manage and overcome imaginary fears to avoid their controlling our lives and impede us from achieving what we want. One of the worst imaginary fears is the fear of failure. This causes a person to fail even before confronting the situation. However, the most feared, even more than death, is stage fright mainly the fear to speak in public. When this begins to interfere with our professional careers, we began to look for a way of managing it and continue with our lives.

Secondary Emotions
Secondary emotions come from a repertoire of learned conducts over time. Secondary emotions are formed by one or more emotions and one or more thoughts. These always derived from the primary emotions. For example, from happiness, love and pleasure are formed; and from sadness, pessimism and sorrow are formed. While, hate, bitterness and impotency are formed from anger. In the same way, anguish, worry, depression and anxiety are formed from fear; and jealousy is formed from anger, sadness and fear.

Many of these secondary emotions originate with the personal interaction of people. In other words, these emotions are not a product of a stimulus like in the case of primary emotions, but are born as a reaction to the behavior of another person. Regardless of how secondary emotions initiate, our thoughts can maintain or increment them indefinitely.

There are secondary emotions like resentment, pessimism, attachment, and hate that can last an entire lifetime. Given the immensely negative impact that these emotions have in the life of a person, it is worth it to give them a look in order to make them disappear.

Positive and Negative Emotions

If our feelings were healthy and our thoughts based on reason, our emotions would be adequate to fulfill their legitimate function, which is to help us survive and confront life with success. Emotions should be balanced in order to feel circumstances in a proper way. Emotions should not fall under the point of balance nor be above it. Having it below, is to not live a circumstance according to reality, while having it above is to live the circumstance with more intensity than what it reality merits. As it is well known, extremes are hardly ever good. In this sense we can say that when emotions are adequate and balanced, they are positive, otherwise, they will only be negative.

For example, if a person feels fear of a poisonous snake, this emotion is adequate and helps him survive. You can say that the emotion is positive. But, if the fear is of a cockroach, the emotion is inadequate and is considered negative. Inadequate emotions can result in a mental and physical disorder.

Management of Emotions

In order to understand our emotions it is necessary to know how our brain functions when we feel, think, or imagine; something that has been made possible thanks to the latest scientific studies on emotions. The more we get to know about emotions, the better capacity we will have to understand them and even come to control them. When we achieve this, then we will become emotionally intelligent.

Given that, emotions are repeated over and over throughout evolutionary history, they have remained recorded in the emotional data bank of our brain as innate or automatic tendencies. Emotions are impulses to react to any situation that is presented to us. With each emotion, the brain prepares the organism for a different type of answer.

When feeling fear, our brain prepares us, so that the greatest amount of the blood goes to the leg muscles, enhancing one's ability to flee. Blood stops circulating through the face, which becomes pale. The brain emits instructions to some glands to release a torrent of hormones that puts the body on maximum alert, preparing it for action and concentrating its attention on the threat. When feeling anger, blood flows to the hands to make them quicker to better attack an enemy. Heart rate is elevated, and a surge of hormones such as adrenaline; generate in the body the energy necessary to produce an action of protection, which is sufficiently strong.

Now, when feeling sadness, the brain helps us adapt to a significant loss, like the death of a loved one, or a great deception. Sadness produces a drop in energy, which slows the metabolism of the organism and diminishes the enthusiasm for the activities in life, especially for entertainments and pleasures and can even turn into depression as it deepens.

When feeling pleasure, on the contrary, the brain impedes negative feelings from surfacing that generate disturbing thoughts and the energy of the body is used instead to create a happy situation that puts the organism into tranquility and relaxation. It also offers a good disposition and enthusiasm to confront any task that presents itself and to give you the ability to achieve many things.

We should adequately manage our emotions so that they last only sufficiently enough to resolve a situation that has presented itself, especially fear, anger, and sadness. If they are unnecessarily prolonged, they can cause health problems, since when the organism prepares the body to respond to the emotion, the effort it makes represents certain wear that if prolonged for a long amount of time or is too frequent, it can become a disorder.

For example, constant fear, which generally is irrational or imaginary, causes anxiety, anguish and stress. Our nervous system connects with the immune system and they as a consequence, are both connected to our emotions. This is why during stressful situations hormones are released, which have a negative impact on our immune system by debilitating the cells in the system, which in turn produces health problems.

Prolonged anger has a devastating effect on the cardiovascular system elevating blood pressure. Each episode of anger adds additional tension to the heart increasing its cardiac rhythm and blood pressure. When this is repeated over and over, it can cause damage to the circulatory system. Of course, if angry people already suffer from cardiac illnesses, anger can have a lethal result. Aggressive people that are easily angered have a higher probability of suffering cardiac arrest than those with more calm temperaments. Having high levels of cholesterol mixed with an aggressive temperament increases the risk.

People that experience prolonged periods of sadness are more prone to fall into a depression. A disproportionate depression is perhaps the emotion that causes the most illnesses and the one that makes recovery more difficult. This is due to the fact that this emotion compromises immunological response. Depression prevents people who suffer from illnesses from being able to overcome them

The negative effects of anger, anxiety, and depression cannot be hidden. These emotions, when chronic, can make people more prone to a series of illnesses. Positive emotions like laughter and happiness can be healing, even changing the course of a grave illness.

It is clear that emotions can affect our health because they are part of our body. This is the reason why when we treat illnesses, we should not separate the body from its emotions, but instead see them as parts of a whole. In fact, medicine would be much more effective in the prevention, as well as in the treatment of illnesses, if the physical state of people could be treated in union with their emotional state. It could be more powerful to use the mind of the patient to cure him, like Jesus would do, than any other medication.

Formation of an Emotion

Before trying to control emotions, it is important to know how they form. This knowledge can alert us about what happens in our body, so this way we can be in a better position to manipulate them until we can control them.

The amygdala is a part of the limbic system that is related to the formation of emotions, since it deals with the management of memories. In the amygdala, the emotions are registered from where the brain accesses them and makes them surface as memories. The more intense the emotion, the stronger the memory will be.

An emotion begins to form when the amygdala sends nervous alarms in response to a determined situation. However, at times, those alarms sent to respond to a present situation, are based on memories that the amygdala has recorded of similar situations, which have occurred in the past. The present results could be completely different than the past situation and this is where the problem herein lies. The most common emotions formed this way are fear and anger.

For example, the formation of an anger emotion ends with the respective overflow, which starts when the heartbeats increase above the normal rhythm of that person in a state of rest. If the cardiac rhythm reaches 100 beats per minutes, which can easily occur during those moments of anger, the organism is pumping adrenaline and other hormones into the bloodstream, which maintain during some time an extended state of anguish.

At that moment when the cardiac rhythm starts to elevate, the muscles tense, which can result in difficulty breathing. An inundation of toxic feelings is produced, and a torrent of anger fear, which look like inevitable and hard to overcome. At this point, the emotion is so intense, that it distorts perspective on the situation and generates confusing thoughts, which alienates any possibility of using reason and logic to abort the overflow and the anger emotion forms.

Controlling Emotions

One of the emotions that we should try to control is fear, especially irrational fear due to the enormous impact it has on our lives. In fact, this type of fear is considered the worst enemy of humanity. To control irrational fear, we should first accept and admit that we feel it. Denying it or ignoring it will not make it disappear. Then, we should analyze it to determine the probability of this fear to converting into a real threat. We should also project a worst-case scenario, to then decide whether the fear can be managed or overcome. After this analysis, perhaps the fear can stop being as terrible as it was at the beginning. Finally, we should confront fear without fear.

A quality that helps us overcome our fears is courage or valor, which is not something we are born with, but can learn to develop. Courage is the mental and emotional preparation and the capacity to confront difficult or daunting situations. It could also mean the capacity to confront fear, pain, danger, uncertainty, intimidation, and other threats. Courage enables us to overcome barriers in order to accomplish the things we need to do.

A great factor in the development of courage is to have faith in one self and in God that all things will come out fine. The confidence that faith gives comes from maintaining a positive attitude and from the visualization of a favorable outcome. A courageous attitude is the product of faith, self-confidence and positive thinking.

Emotions in the right proportion are necessary because they help us resolve the situations for which they were designed. The problem comes when the emotions are disproportionate in time, place, and objective. To maintain inadequate or negative emotions under control is the key to emotional wellbeing. When these emotions grow with too much intensity or during a lengthy amount of time, they lessen our stability.

Even though controlling an emotion in full development is not an easy task, especially if we are talking about rage, or even worse in its most elevated stage; anger. But, it is possible after an emotional experience, to learn for the next time. To better illustrate this point I will tell you that once I saw someone get so angry that he looked like he had transformed into a monster, all because a little dog had eaten the food that someone had stored away in the kitchen. He took a stick bigger and harder than a baseball bat and threw it at its head, killing the dog, right in front of his girlfriend and her mother.

Perhaps if this person had been facing a tiger, his anger could have been justified since the tiger is big and very strong and could have killed him, but a little dog that barely reached his knee could not do any harm to him. Besides, the dog was not mad, it was just taking a nap from her little meal. This was an episode of disproportionate anger. The emotion surpassed the point of equilibrium and besides that, the object did not merit that emotion with such intensity.

On the other hand, the individual was very loved by this girlfriend and her family. They never thought he could be so cruel, and of course, after killing the defenseless animal, the girlfriend and part of his friends left him. I do not blame them, since someone that lashes out with such disproportionate anger against a little dog, can also do the same to a person. Another important aspect in this situation is that the emotion of the individual did not manifest itself at the adequate moment.

Let's examine the situation that produced such anger; a plate of food that was probably cold already had been eaten. Perhaps if this dog had killed the mother or the girlfriend of the individual, but not even in that case could such violence be justified. We then see that that inadequate emotion did not have a cause to substantiate it.

From an experience like this, a person; of course, after calming down, reflecting and analyzing the situation, could learn from the disparate emotion in regard to its cause, intensity and time. For this, it is required to accept the reality of the situation just as it happened and not try to justify his acts. It also requires having the sufficient will to do it. But one thing is for sure; if he is capable of learning from one past experience he will continue learning from subsequent ones until he can manage to produce adequate emotions.

There are other emotions, which even have no reason to exist. Like those that occur to people, when they are driving their car, especially in the middle of traffic. Sometimes the person could be calmly in his car, but all it takes is for them to believe someone has cut them off, or passed them too closely, or looked at them in a rude way, to start insulting the other driver and yell all kinds of inappropriate things at them. There are some people that even use graphic language and make offensive gestures to the other driver they believe is bothering them. They reach a rage of such high proportion; they begin to hit the steering wheel or dashboard of the car. If someone calls them on the telephone at that moment, they would answer without any courtesy and with obscenities.

Even worst is that the other person that they suppose caused such rage is not even aware of what is happening, arriving calmly at his destination, while the enraged one arrives stressed, anguished, bad humored, and even with high tension. This situation is fairly common in people. Now, is there any reason for this? The answer is simply, no. That is an emotion without any objective or sense totally unnecessary and avoidable.

Another important thing we can do to manage our emotions is to get rid of our negative thoughts, like we have recommended in subchapter 1.4 in the section on "Managing Worries", parts 4 and 5. Negative thoughts distort our reality and submerge us into pessimism. This produces a mood of weariness, which can cause us see the world worse than it is. This could distort our emotions by making them disproportionate.

To control our emotions, we must control their impulses, which have a normal tendency to externalize very quickly. The ability to control the impulse is the solid base for the will and character. Not controlling the impulse converts us into emotional people, expressing our emotions without any type of measure of consequences incurring errors and even offenses against other people. In these cases, emotions guide our steps as if we thought with our heart when in reality what should guide our life is the wise part of the mind, as if we thought with our brain.

Not having any control over our emotions has been a problem for many years. In fact, it is believed that the emission of the first codes of laws of ancient times, like the Ten Commandments, was made with the intention to dominate emotions.

People should control their emotions to be more tolerant when faced with frustration, and calm their anger, expressing it in a more adequate way; having a less aggressive behavior, manage stress better; and have more positive feelings about themselves, their family and the society they are a part of. In this way people will be more responsible, will have a greater capacity to pay attention and concentrate in the search for solutions to their problems, be less impulsive, and have more self-control.

In conclusion, controlling emotions does not mean suppressing them, since they are necessary and fulfill a great role in our lives by helping us resolve situations. It signifies having balanced emotions so that they do not tear our lives apart. When we manage to learn to control our thoughts in order to generate more adequate emotions, as well as, to learn from our past emotions in their sense of being, cause, intensity, objective, time and form, then we would have taken a big step in the path of emotional intelligence. After all, is this not what Daniel Goldman refers to in the Aristotle's challenge?

3.3 Thought

Humans are rational beings that, thanks to its thinking have come to understand the world. Likewise, the human being can, through his thinking, cultivate in himself the important qualities to develop the attitude that would permit him to obtain his happiness. However, today, we see that that great thinking that gave us so many achievements has degenerated, becoming negative in the majority of the people. In order to take back our good thoughts, we must change the bad ones. This is possible to do by knowing how the thought emerged, evolved and how thinking functions in our mind to eradicate negatives thoughts and embrace with a sense of urgency, a new more advanced way of thinking in order to think positively and thus recuperate the lost advances of our past.

How Did Thinking Emerge?

Thinking emerged from the perception and interpretation that man began to have about his external world. The perceived sensation can be pleasing or displeasing. Generally we are always more interested in experiencing pleasurable sensations and avoiding the ones that are not pleasurable. This interest is what released the mechanism of reason and thinking.

When we touch another body, we can perceive its form, texture, temperature and other properties. In this case, the contact indicates to us that those sensations come from the body that we touched around us. All the perceptions we receive from the exterior world represent ideas, which can be sensory or intellectual. Sensory ideas show us the objects we perceive in that same moment. While, the intellectual ideas are recorded in our memory and we access them when the objects are not found before us.

It is believed that sensations are the source of all the thoughts, with which we form judgments of value over our environment. As a result, we can consider that all that emerges from our mind is a thought.

Evolution of Thinking

At the beginning, thinking was very logical since it was based on reason. This type of thoughts helped us analyze situations in order to find solutions to adverse events. As logical thinking went evolving and after our ancestors developed imagination more than 170 thousand years ago, thinking entered a new age of advancement and generated creative thinking.

Proof of this progress is that today, we can go back to those times of our ancestors and imagine what could have happened when on one of their outings, they might have taken a big egg and broken it in two. After eating what was on the inside, they began to stare at both halves and decided to use them for drinking water.

Bingo! An act, perhaps as simple as this, could have marked the glory of the human being, since with the image that we have of an object we can visualize in our mind the actions we want to take to later modify that object. In other words, the human being could now transfer his future actions that were only in his mind. Transferring an action into mental images indicates that: thinking. In effect, thinking is the faculty of having mental images and creating relations with these images. In this way, the human being began to think within himself and later to utilize language as a means to communicate his thoughts to other people.

Thinking has evolved throughout the years. Thanks to our intelligence and our ability to adapt, we have conquered the world utilizing thinking as the great tool, which can permit us to find answers, resolve problems, and invent. Thinking started to be utilized then by modern society with Socrates; the great Greek philosopher that lived between the years 470 BC to 399 BC. Socrates was considered the father of modern thinking. Afterwards, other Greek philosophers of the same era Plato and Aristotle continued the work of Socrates.

At the beginning, the majority of our thoughts were positive and based on reason since the majority of the human beings had a similar reality. As our knowledge increased, our ability to think also expanded and we became creative. Back then, the relationship between the knowledge and the ability to think was in balance.

However; with the passing of time, a variety of new experiences was emerging, especially with the arrival of shamanism, a type of belief practiced by some humans called Shamans over 50 thousand years ago, to cure human suffering with the help of spirits. This later on unfurled into what we know as religion. With shamanism, emerged many thoughts that knowledge could not give an answer to. During and after this period of beliefs and spiritual practice, human beings began to have contact with hallucinogenic substances and began experiencing altered states of consciousness. Of course, this also altered their thoughts and much of these people began to distort what until then, had been the common reality, which introduced dramatic changes in their thoughts.

This different thinking began to divide humans. The new reality of that minority incorporated aspects somewhat distant from real reality, and their thoughts moved away from the logical creating a series of limitations for achieving the things required to lead a better life. Thinking then became negative since far from helping them see solutions; it led them to more problems.

Currently, the tendency towards negative thinking has increased to the point that more than 70% of the world population has embraced it without realizing it. This is the reason why humanity is in a situation of poverty and hopelessness, which will lead them through the wrong path. The solution is simple; go back to our positive, logical, and creative thinking to get back on the path to prosperity.

In conclusion, thinking can be defined as any product, real or imaginary, of the mind. The activity of thinking or generating a thought should be based on reason, knowledge, memory, comprehension and imagination. Thinking has the particularity of giving existence in the mind to things that in reality do not exist. Another particularity that thinking has is that it generates thoughts according to how a person perceives or interprets what he thinks is real. In other words, if the interpretation of his reality is distorted, his thinking will also be distorted.

Positive and Negative Thoughts

When thinking is guided using reason, it is known as logical, which helps us to reason in order to solve problems. When thinking helps us create things or generate new ideas, it is called creative. All thoughts that are logical and creative ones are of great use since they better our quality of life and are considered positive. While any other thinking that does not help us in any way is considered negative and unnecessary.

Today, we generally live in a state of constant thinking. Each day we think about what we are going to do today, tomorrow, or in the future. How things will turn out for us, will depend on how we think. In order for things to go well, our thoughts need to be positive. You may be asking yourself; how do we know what type of thoughts we are producing? In general when we are not happy since we have not achieved what we want, is because our thoughts are not positive, or at least, are not guided towards what we want to achieve.

How is it that we produce positive or negative thoughts? When we think that we will come out of a situation successfully, we are generating a positive thought which will lead us to success. But on the contrary, if we were afraid of confronting the situation, then we would be generating a negative thought. We will not achieve what we want. In many cases, we do not even produce the thought, for it is already in our subconscious mind. Some of those thoughts come from our childhood, from things that happened at a very early age and that hurt us and marked us with feelings of failure.

After this entire exposition, we see the importance of positive thoughts, which should be logical and creative. These are necessary to achieve everything in life, even to have good health. On the other hand, we understand that negative thoughts - which far from helping us - bring us more problems. These thoughts are derived from false ideas that were created in our minds due to lack of information and certain beliefs. Negative thoughts can distort reality, which is why we should change them to positive ones by following the instructions found in points 4 and 5 of the section "Management of Worries" from subchapter 1.4.

How Thoughts Function In the Mind

Thoughts function in our minds like a seed we plant in a garden. If the seed is good, a good plant will grow which will bear good fruit for our benefit and the benefit of our own. If on the contrary, the seed is bad, a bad plant will grow which will bear bad fruits.

In the same way, if we plant in our mind, (garden), a positive thought, (seed), we will then obtain a reflection of a positive action for us and our own. If on the contrary, we plant a negative thought, we will obtain the reflection of a negative action in return. We constantly think and almost always, our thoughts come to our mind without us realizing it. We have to be conscious of our thoughts in order to identify them and be able to manage them for our convenience. It is important to remember that only positive thoughts will help us achieve the things we want.

Advanced Thinking

Each and every one of us are a product of our thoughts which are molded throughout our lives with the experiences we live, our upbringing, our beliefs, our education, and the environment which surrounds us. These thoughts form a pattern that defines our way of being and acting. In other words, our thoughts program our mind to be who we are. This is why I insist, that we are what we think, and to be good our thoughts should also be good.

A great part of our way of thinking is learned; therefore, we can change it. Most of our thought occurs subconsciously, and our conscious thoughts constitute a small portion of our mind's activity. Whatever the case may be, when we think, we will always do it on the basis of thoughts that we already have registered in our mind. In fact, if we generate a new thought, it will be affected by our way of thinking. Here is the importance of thinking positively in order to produce better thoughts so they can help us achieve our objective in life, which is none other than to achieve success and to be happy.

However, we see with the passing of years, perhaps from so much uncertainty over the stability of our countries, or for whatever other reason, that negative thoughts in people are increasing and have become the traditional way of thinking. A thought full of negativity and falsehoods do not help in any way, do not provide any solutions, and only lead to more problems. Negative thoughts have stopped the success of people and will continue to do so for the rest of their lives unless they do something about it now to change them. All of the problems of humanity today are a product of their traditional way of thinking. To resolve these problems one should use a more advanced thinking.

Like a computer, our brain needs us to update its "software". For a computer to do all the tasks that is expected of it each day, it needs to operate with a system of Windows 7 or something more advanced. It is almost impossible to do it with a system of Windows 3.1. In the same manner, we should, with a sense of urgency, reprogram our mind with a system of thoughts more advanced than the traditional. An advanced thought would help us use our mind how we really should in order to achieve what we most want in life.

Everything we achieve or do not achieve in life will depend on our way of thinking. If a person has not achieved what they want in their life, this is the moment to change their thoughts. When we speak of a more advanced way of thinking we are referring precisely to eradicating negative thoughts and promoting positive thinking just as we have seen. We can learn to change our negative thoughts into positive ones, which will help us be successful in all aspects of our life. The only thing that impedes a person from achieving success is the person himself.

In order to develop higher thinking, we should see things as they are. In other words, we should get our personal reality more in tune with the real reality, and for this, it is very important to revise our beliefs and make the necessary changes. In this sense, it is recommended to go to subchapter 4.3 and review the topic of beliefs to see their impact on the reality of a person. People think according to their beliefs. If their beliefs are positive then their thoughts will also be positive and this serves to help them achieve their objective in life, while if their beliefs are negative, then their thoughts will be the same which will only limit the person's capacity for achievement.

Beliefs affect our reality and at the same time this affects the perception we have of ourselves, and the world around us. A person's reality defines the confidence he has in himself. Each person is unique and sees the world in a unique way; this is why personal reality varies with the person. If his reality is based on negative experiences or on negative interpretations of past experiences, that reality will not help him achieve the things he wants. Our perception of things will depend on our reality.

Our perception is another important aspect in the development of positive thinking. Our way of reacting emotionally, to the words or gestures of other people, depend on how we perceive them. Sometimes an emotion makes a person happy, but the same emotion can make another person unhappy. The words or gestures of a person can praise one person yet offend another one. So what matters are not the emotions, words or gestures, but the way in which they are perceived.

Of course, we can also change the perception of things and for this we only need to change the way we see that thing, in other words, see it in a positive way. By changing our perception, we also change our world and what we expect from it. To expect too much from people can produce in us frustration and stress, especially when people do not act how we expect them to. For this reason it is better to lower our expectations and thus have a calmer vision of our world.

Once we have managed to eradicate negative beliefs, we can see more clearly the tangible reality, have a better perception of things, and generate better thoughts. These are the thoughts that permit us to see life with more clarity in order to resolve our problems by ourselves, to see and take opportunities that will lead us to prosperity, and permits us the realization of our dreams, to live a full life.

3.4 Intelligence

To have intelligence is to know how to choose the best option among the ones that we have available to solve a problem. It was always thought that with academic intelligence, the one that permits us to learn in order to graduate from some school, we could obtain all the success necessary in life, but as we have already proven, that type of intelligence by itself is not sufficient to achieve the long sought after goal of happiness.

With the arrival of emotional intelligence it was believed that by using it in combination with the academic intelligence, that success was assured. However, even though this combination helps a lot, it is not enough for achieving what we want in life. The question that arises then is; what else is needed? Besides academic and emotional intelligence, there exists another type of intelligence related with the depth of the subconscious mind called intuitive intelligence. These three types of intelligence should be present in people in order to have the necessary tools to solve problems and respond to the interrogative; what good does it do us to be intelligent?

What Is Intelligence?

Intelligence is the capacity to assimilate, keep, and elaborate information to solve problems. Intelligence is formed by variables like attention, the capacity of observation, memory, learning, and the unique abilities of the individual. Human beings, like animals, come into the world equipped with instincts, which from the very beginning enable them to adapt to life in their natural surroundings, through innate guidelines of behavior that only have to be developed.

Apart from their instincts, each person is born with a certain intellectual capacity inherited from their parents. However, his intelligence will depend on how he or she develops that intellect that nature has endowed them with. Intelligent people generally operate closer to the limit of their intellectual capacity. Of course, this will depend on their personal effort and social environment. Human beings, like some other animals, have the capacity to learn by observing and the capacity to learn by imitation.

Learning is achieved with academic intelligence. However, to have success in life, people also need to control their emotions. This control is achieved with emotional intelligence, but this, although it can help us a lot, does not resolve everything. This has made some people ask themselves if there is something more to intelligence. In effect there is. Apart from academic and emotional intelligence, there exists another type of intelligence known as intuitive intelligence.

Academic Intelligence

For many years, intelligence was equivalent to the use of logical thinking or the ability of a person to reason. It had always been thought that there was only one type of intelligence, which was closely linked with academic learning, and for this reason it had been called academic intelligence, which was what was useful for obtaining good grades in school.

Academic intelligence is the one we inherit form our parents and is measured through the intellectual coefficient or IQ. However, this type of intelligence does not always constitute a guarantee of prosperity or happiness. Academic intelligence does not always proportion success in life, for today we have seen that other aspects like management and control of feelings and emotions are necessary. Academic intelligence does not prepare us to adequately confront the daily situations in life like difficulties or opportunities.

If we wanted to see a profile of the people that are grouped under academic intelligence we would have to see that they are people with a high intellectual coefficient and are normally characterized by being ambitious, productive, predictable, and do not worry much about themselves. Also, these types of people tend to be critical, condescending, inhibited, they feel uncomfortable with sexuality, and are emotionally cold. On the other hand, the profile of people with a high emotional intelligence, indicates that they are socially balanced, sociable and happy, more sure of themselves, responsible, solitary, and careful about their relationships. In general, they are happier since they feel comfortable with themselves, with others, and with the social world where they live.

Both academic intelligence and emotional intelligence are desirable and always coexist intertwined in us. Emotional intelligence can be learned, contrary to academic intelligence, which we inherit from our parents. The fact that we can learn to be emotionally intelligent constitutes without doubt a great hope for people with a low intellectual coefficient, since we can make changes to help ourselves and help others to have a better life.

As we have been able to see throughout history, people with high intellectual coefficient are not always very successful. In fact, it has been determined that the success of people only depends 20% on their academic intelligence. Other 70% depends on their emotional intelligence. Emotional intelligence also influences in the motivation of people, in persisting when confronted with adversity, on being less impulsive, getting along with other people, being more understanding, and even housing hopes.

Emotional Intelligence

Emotional intelligence, a term popularized by Daniel Goleman, is the capacity to know and understand our feelings and emotions with the purpose of managing and controlling them as well as the ability to self-motivate ourselves to increase the possibility of success in life. Given that other people can affect the achieving of what one wants, emotional intelligence also includes our ability to recognize the emotions in others and manage them to have good relationships with them. Even though emotional intelligence is not a gift of nature, we can all develop it if we want to; we only need to see life under a new perspective.

Therefore, to be emotionally intelligent, is to understand the origin of feelings, what is means to have self-awareness, learn emotional management and control, in other words, channel emotions correctly, be able to self-motivate ourselves in order to achieve personal improvement and be able to motivate others. Also, last but not least, to have empathy in order to understand the feelings of others and positively manage our relationships with others in a healthy way, to respect and be respected.

Emotionally intelligent people know and manage their own feelings and efficiently interpret and manage the feelings of others. Besides this, they have great leadership ability, they cultivate and maintain relationships, and they resolve conflicts in their lives, whether it is in a romantic liaison, work, business, or a friendship. The happiest people are those that are gifted with well-developed emotional abilities, which make them, feel satisfied in every activity of their life.

In order to successfully manage relationships with other people, we should have a great empathetic ability. Empathy is the innate ability of human beings to know what another person is feeling. This ability is developed through consciousness of our own emotions, which helps us to interpret feelings. Therefore all rapport or interest for someone surges from our ability to be empathetic.

The rational mind expresses itself through words; however, the expression of emotions is not verbal. Emotions rarely are expressed in words, with much more frequency they are manifested through other signs like tone of voice, gestures, and facial expression.

The development of empathy begins in infancy. In great part it has to do with the education our parents gave us. The empathy of children begins forming by seeing the reaction of others when someone is afflicted and by imitating what they see, they begin to develop their empathy. When the child understands that his emotions are well received, accepted, and corresponded to, he feels understood. From those moments on, the child begins to perceive that other people can share his feelings.

If children stop developing empathy, they become apathetic, which is the opposite of empathy. But the implication of having no sympathy is much more profound, since when parents stop showing empathy over the emotions of the child, like his joys, tears, need for love, the child begins to stop expressing and even from feeling those emotions. If throughout infancy these emotions continue without emerging, they could disappear from the emotional repertoire of the child.

In the same way, children can develop other types of less desirable emotions, depending on the mood of the parents. If they are depressed, especially the mother, who is the one who has more contact with them, children will reflect the mood of their parents showing more feelings of sadness. The treatment that we received as children will be the key to how we will be as adults. However, any imbalance in our way of being that we may have acquired during this stage in life can be corrected later.

It is important to know the concept of empathy to interpret our emotions. It will help us understand the point of view of the other person, perceive his feelings and better our ability to hear the other person. Empathy leads people to follow determined moral principles, which help them be good people. Apart from empathy, it is also required to have self-control in order to manage the emotions of others, which is the essence in the art of managing interpersonal relationships. The absence of these abilities can result in the failure of any person in their relationships with others.

Intuitive Intelligence

Intuition is an innate faculty that we all have in greater or lesser degree, that in certain situations can provide us with immediate knowledge without having to use reason. For example, when we have a "gut feeling" or a thought about something and later it happens, we are using our intuition. The information that is generated during an intuitive perception originates in the deepest part of our subconscious.

Intuitive perceptions can be physically manifested through certain sensations in the body, like a heartbeat, associated with something that perhaps is happening in another place, to another person or that will happen in the future. These perceptions can also be manifested through emotions. There are people that can feel sad or happy in the anticipation of something that will happen. The other way in which intuitive perceptions can manifest themselves is through the mind, through the reception of thoughts and ideas of something that the person could be doing, like something creative.

Intuition is simply the internal voice that sometimes tries to tell us which road to follow, or that warns us of something that is going to happen. Intuition is the sixth sense that lights up our conscious mind to take us through the better path. Clearly, the more quiet and harmonious our mind is, and the more positive our thoughts are, the greater the possibility we will have to hear this small voice inside of us.

Now, our capacity to perceive, interpret and use the information contained in our intuition to make important decisions in our lives, is what is known as intuitive intelligence, which represents the other 10% of the success of people. Intuitive intelligence also permits us to search deep in our subconscious, for answers and solutions to any situation or problem, which would surface in the form of intuition. Intuitive intelligence is innate but it can also be cultivated.

What Good Does It Do To Us To Be Intelligent?

Some people, after having read the previous section on intelligence and the different types, could ask themselves: "So then, how many types of intelligence do we have to develop in order to have what we want in life?" They can continue arguing that before having only one type of intelligence was sufficient.

With academic intelligence it was assumed that a person could go to school and pursue a career in which he could make enough money to live well, and educate his children, in other words, have certain happiness. They later continued arguing; they said that type of intelligence was not sufficient so we needed another type of intelligence that would help us manage and control emotions. Thus, the argument continues; now we see that the so-called emotional intelligence is not sufficient either, and they tell us that we must also have intuitive intelligence. So finally they exclaim, My God!

Other people could object to the need for so much intelligence. Especially when they think that before in order to be the manager of a company a person would had to have studied and had some experience; however, now any one can be a manager. Not only this, before to be president of any country, one had to be an exemplary citizen with all the levels of education possible, these days, anyone can be president. They have power and everything they want. Therefore, people could be asking and with much reason; what good does it do to us to be intelligent?

It's true that the things we see daily, cause questions like these to arise. It would seem that merits and values are no longer important, and that the people would be religiously following the bad. It is precisely that immense lack of talent in the spheres of power, which has led us into chaos. Trying to explain a bit about what is happening in regards to the question of intelligence, we can say that the entire problem began when corruption passed from the public sector to the private one, which brought as a result, more power to the politicians. So much that they began to have certain control in the private sector which began to contaminate it with them.

We can also say that academic intelligence was represented by the private sector until the politicians came converted into the magicians of emotions, making them overflow to the maximum in order to later capitalize them and rise in power. The politicians manipulated parts of the private sector, the business class, as well as its workers and they became their allies.

Now something to reflect on: if the people that without a doubt were academically intelligent had been emotionally intelligent, the world we live in today would be different. If they had combined these two types of intelligence they would have been able to manage and control their emotions, so as not to fall into the trap of politicians allowing them to conserve the conquests, owed to their academic intelligence, and we would have a much different world today. This reflection can help us understand the importance of having and combining academic and emotional intelligence.

However, some people may be asking: and what about the other type of intelligence, the intuitive one, is it of any use to us? It is of great use! We should excavate the most profound area of our subconscious mind until we find God, so that through our intuition, he can help us have the necessary wisdom to overcome this mess in which the politicians have gotten us into and bring back the values and good habits that one day made us prosperous and happy beings.

In conclusion, we see that each day we should be much more intelligent in order to confront with success each new experience. Thank God we have all the intelligence we need to move forward. We also see how these three types of intelligence are necessary to achieve our happiness and the happiness of our people.

3.5 Mental Health

We have said that the brain is the most important organ of the human body. The reason for this is because there resides the human mind, which controls all the other parts of the body. If ancient Egyptians would have understood this simple and important concept, they would have conserved the brain intact in their mummies and thus they would have achieved immortality, something they sought for a long time. To understand the importance of the mind is the key to giving it the appropriate nutrition to keep it healthy. Now, it is also very important to know that the mind is fed with our thoughts. Therefore, they better be good ones.

One of the greatest things that a person should desire in life is to have a healthy body and a healthy mind. This, of course, can come from the famous phrase, "healthy body in a healthy mind". However, it is worth stressing that it is much more important to have a healthy mind, since the mind is the one that will direct our body through the paths of life. If we have a healthy mind, it can help us heal our body, which is not possible if it were the other way around.

We have seen physically well-formed bodies; completely beautiful bodies that look that they could have been sculpted by the ancient Greeks, but sometimes result being very fragile and not healthy. That can be fixed, however, as long as the mind is healthy. For this, we resort to a good nutritional diet and exercises like we saw in the section about body health. Now, to maintain a healthy mind is something totally different. It would appear that it would be much easier to feed and train the body than it is to train and feed the mind. However, this really isn't so. If it seem like this is the case, it is because we do not yet know how to do it.

We feed the body with food and we train it with physical exercise. We feed the mind with thoughts and we train it with mental exercises. The better the food and physical exercise, the better the body will be. In the same way, the better our thoughts are, the healthier our mind will be. A healthy mind is achieved with positive thoughts so they can lead us to positive situations. Now, positive thoughts should also be logical. Thinking that tomorrow we will go to the planet Mercury to look for gold, would seem positive, but it is not logical, since it makes no sense. Logical thinking channels positive thinking - to make it more effective - in achieving what we want.

If our mind is healthy, we should not feel any irrational fear, nor be so susceptible to pain, nor have any type of complexes or prejudgments. If our mind is healthy, we can better confront suffering so that it will not tear at our soul, to be stronger so we don't fall into temptations, to forgive those who have offended us and have a better perspective so we can be more prosperous for our own good as well as to help our neighbor.

We are a product of our thoughts, therefore they should be positive, since they bring us our happiness, while negative thoughts only generate unnecessary suffering, perturb our personality, and make relationships with other people more difficult. In order to have good mental and emotional health, as it is now called, we should cultivate positive thinking and eradicate the negativity. Positive thoughts are healthy, stabilize our emotions, and produce profitable moods, while negative thoughts are harmful and can distort the emotional activity, which generates altered states of mood.

A mind that mostly generates positive thoughts is of course a healthy mind and allows us to have a clear vision of situations which is known as mental lucidity. On the other hand, a mind that generates negative thoughts is an obfuscated mind, creating confusion in people. The obfuscation gives the mind a distorted use of the imagination, the interpretation of the situation and the way it responds.

Only in the measure with which one trains to see with clarity, beyond the distorted influence of obfuscation, can it perceive and appreciate the world with wisdom. An obscured mind is a seedbed of negative thoughts from which surge so many negative emotions.

Just as many times it is not possible to exercise any type of control over circumstance or external situations, it is possible to do so in regard to our moods, emotions and thoughts. In order to have good mental health, we should learn to modify our attitude in life, control our thoughts, and stimulate factors of interior growth to increase clarity, promote positive emotions, and adequately confront the situations in the world around us. We should also resolve emotional internal conflicts, stabilize our emotional activity, overcome frustrations, solve the traumas and repressions, have good self-esteem, overcome unnecessary worries, anguish and irrational fear, identify and eradicate negative thoughts, and cultivate positive thinking.

In the society in which we live, we are subjected to a lot of negative influence, which is why we should move with much mental balance to avoid being infected. It is very important to control our thinking and this requires our conscious attention, with which we can better observe our negative emotions so we don't express them or at least try to rectify them.

Our world today is full of calamities, poverty, envy, greed, confusion, stress, anxiety, depression, and hate. This makes people generate many negative thoughts, especially if their mind is disorganized and without any control. Negative thoughts contaminate our mind, which has a perturbing effect on people. A contaminated mind is confused and cannot have clarity or lucidity to help people confront their problems with success. To decontaminate the mind is to get rid of all its toxic thoughts. Now, liberating the mind is the art of thinking or not thinking, of mentally connecting or not connecting when you want to. In other words, it means to have control over the mind. It is to be oneself with our thoughts: good or bad and see them coming, remain for a while and then leave, without it affecting us, much less tear apart our soul. Just like the white or black clouds; they come, they stay for a while, and then they leave without affecting the sky or tearing it apart. It is here where meditation plays a great role.

Meditation is the way to train the mind so we can start to exercise control over it, providing it attention, equity, calmness and harmony. One of the most popular methods of meditation is the one in a sitting position, which requires a quiet place, if possible, where a stable position can be maintained, with the spinal cord and the head erect and trying to obtain the best possible immobility. The eyes can be closed or semi-open. You have to constantly try to develop your capacity for concentration, avoiding all possible distractions. Breathing should be, preferably, through the nose and a bit slow and paused. You should maintain a firm mind even though physical discomforts may arise or disturbing mental states. Meditation, even if only practiced for a few minutes daily, is a good way to strengthen the will and gain healthy dominion over the mind. Even though we cannot control the circumstance around us, we can control our mind to keep it healthy.

4. Life Is a Matter of Attitude

In the previous chapter we continued with the knowledge of our body, centering our attention on the wonderful human mind, to closely know how this wonder called the mind functions, after been forged during a long process of evolution. We studied our emotions and thoughts, as well as the way to manage them so they can help us in our daily living. We saw how and why we should be more intelligent in order to follow in the good path of life and the importance of having a healthy mind so it can guide us through life.

In this chapter we will cover the necessary topics for the development of an attitude that will permit us to make the difficult task of living much easier. Attitude is the way a person acts towards life. When one has a good attitude, a person can achieve the things he wants. That is why we say that life is a matter of attitude. In order to achieve this attitude, we need to develop a set of tendencies over important aspects in our life that are required to achieve happiness, such as having a good personality, having positive beliefs, and becoming a good friend.

The learning and development of the attitude toward life initiates in childhood where the formation of the personality begins. Personality is in great part tied to the success in life of people. Beliefs, is another important factor in developing a good attitude since from them, the reality of the person and his perception of himself and the world will depend. Of course, it is also important to be a good friend since this helps the person work with people, for people, and through people, which is the key to the development of a good attitude. Also, in order to have the correct attitude toward life and achieve the things required to live life fully, people should also be optimistic, have faith, hope, develop a positive attitude about money, have a good sense of humor, and be free from vices.

4.1 The Learning Stage

From the day we are born into this world, we begin the learning stage, which we can achieve thanks to the feeling of love we develop from the link with our mother during pregnancy. The learning stage continues until our final healthy days. After our first 7 months, we learn the two most important things of human beings; talking and walking. The rest of the things that we accomplish in life will depend on them. Standing and later walking by our own means gives us *confidence* in ourselves since we feel capable of controlling our body. By talking, apart from the confidence, it also shows us our *capacity for communication*. These two aptitudes bring about *self-control*.

Interacting with our environment will require us to learn to manage our emotions. Emotional learning begins in the first moments of life and is prolonged throughout infancy. The interchanges between parents and children mold the emotional learning of the child, since the messages of their parents are ingrained in the memory of the child and will repeat throughout the years. Therefore, the relationship between parents and child should be very positive so the child can start to adequately manage his emotions and thus be able to develop the correct attitude towards life. Children of immature parents, who consume drugs, are depressed, lack goal, and lead chaotic lives, will be negatively affected in the onset of their attitude.

During the first three years of the life of a child, his brain grows to approximately two thirds of its definite size and evolves in complexity at a rate greater than he will ever reach. During this period, learning is more accelerated than in earlier years, and emotional learning comes to be of great importance. Also, during these first years, a great stress can damage the learning centers of the brain and thus damage the intellect. As you can see, the impact of this first learning stage is very critical

Already at 7 years old, generally we have learned how to read and write. Oh! How good it would be if we also learned to pay attention. At this age we already go to school, church and visit places. This means, that besides interacting with our parents and family members, we also do it with our teachers and classmates, the people in church, and our friends.

Our first 7 years are extremely important in our development, as people, because everything we learn throughout this period from the people we have interacted with, have been put in our mind in the form of thoughts. Those thoughts will remain imprinted in our brain to later indicate to us how to act in a specific situation. This way of thinking will determine the personality that we will have as an adult and the one that will mark the attitude we will develop towards life.

As a consequence, it is highly necessary that our parents and family members that interact with us, like the teacher, the pastor, and friends, have good thoughts. This is so that we can develop the correct attitude towards life and achieve all that is necessary to attain what we want from it. Otherwise, our life could be destined to confront many difficult situations, unless we learn later how to make the necessary changes to modify it.

The way, in which parents treat their children, whether it is with discipline, empathy, comprehension, indifference, or love, has profound and lasting consequences in the emotional life of the child. Better yet, if the parents are emotionally intelligent, the benefit to the child will be immense. These parents are more effective when trying to help their children through emotional ups and downs, since they are parents that pay attention to the feelings of their children, utilizing these emotional moments as an opportunity to get close to them and help them in the learning stage of their emotions. Furthermore, emotionally intelligent parents, not only listen respectfully to what bothers their children, but also allow them to express their emotions freely and openly.

Children that learn to better manage their own emotions are the most effective ones in trying to calm themselves down when they are worried and they worry less frequently. They are also less stressed and more sociable; they can pay more attention and concentrate better, which has a positive impact even on their intellectual coefficient.

As adults, we learn to understand a bit more of our world, thanks to the learning that occurs during these years. After the age of 27, we should already have learned enough to know what we want in life. By then, we should have formed the necessary values to develop personality and achieve the correct attitude towards life.

4.2 Personality

A great part of a person's success is linked to their personality, which is normally formed and developed during infancy. A part of our personality we inherit from our parents and the other part we take from the environment in which we develop. Personality depends a lot on temperament and character. There are some types of temperament that benefit personality while others don't. But this is no longer a problem since we can change the temperament that comes in our genes. As far as character, it can also be changed more easily because it is learned.

Another important factor in personality is constituted by self-esteem, or the value that a person assigns to himself. This is of great importance to people, since what they accomplish in life will depend on their self-esteem. In order to have good personality, besides having a good temperament, good character, and self-esteem, people should concentrate on being friendly, respectful, nice, open minded, emotionally stable, and have a good sense of humor. A good personality is vital in our lives, since it will be the key that will open the door to happiness.

Formation and Development of Personality

Personality is defined as the typical pattern of thinking, feeling, and behavior in a human being, which is what makes him unique. This pattern tends to remain stable throughout the life of a person, unless this person has the sufficient courage and knowledge to modify it. Contrary to what was once believed, nowadays, we know that we can make the necessary changes to our personality so that it can help us achieve the things we want.

In the formation of personality, a part of it is genetically inherited and the rest we take from the environment in which we develop. From our very first months of life, we begin to differentiate from other children. For example, we can see that some children are more attentive or active than others, differences that can later influence their behavior. Among the characteristics of inherited personality are academic intelligence and temperament.

The other part of personality that we take from our surrounding environment is developed throughout the years, especially during childhood because of the influence of other people in our environment like our parents, teachers, pastors, and friends. The influence of people in our environment will have a very important impact in the development of our beliefs and values. As we grow, our own experiences in life will also influence in a resolute way, our own personality, as well as our socioeconomic status and other factors like race, religion, and culture.

The family environment is perhaps the most important component in the development of our personality. We learn from the behavior of our parents, since through their own behaviors, they expose situations that produce certain conduct in their children, with which they can come to identify with. We also learn from the evaluation that our parents make of our behavior. This way, we can see that they reward us when we adopt a behavior that they assume is correct or they punish us when we behave in a contrary way. We also learn from the behavior of our brothers and sisters, especially if they are older. They, like our parents, also become role models for us.

Friends and companions from childhood and adolescence, and later those at work and other social groups during adulthood also influence our personality. Personality will depend very closely on temperament, beliefs, values, and the intelligence of the person.

Temperament

Our temperament is the set of traits or characteristics that we have genetically inherited from our parents and is defined as the natural way in which a person responds to his emotions to interact and live with the surrounding environment. Temperament affects all the actions and reactions in life, including the ability to adapt to changes, the mood and the intensity with which we live, which in turn, will depend on the magnitude with which an emotion or feeling is experienced. From this, we learn the degree of emotionalism and passion in people. In other words, if the person is happy frequently, a little, or never, and if by doing it he sweats, gets red, the voice trembles, gets pale, or cold.

The way in which we perceive things internally and emotionally is also an indication of the intensity with which we respond to emotion and the type of temperament of the person. Intense responses are common in unstable or strong temperaments while the less intense responses are generally common in weaker temperaments. Other indicators of intense temperament, whether strong or weak, are the tone and volume of the voice, as well as, the energy with which a hand is shaken, or the pressure that is put on the paper when writing.

The duration of the emotional response generated by a situation, also speaks of the temperament of the person. There are people that get very excited, but just as quickly they become unexcited, while others do it with less intensity, but their emotion lasts longer. Another important aspect of temperament is how much stimulation a person needs to emit an emotional response. People with little stimulation, are more sensitive and require less stimuli to react, in fact, even for intense reactions. While other people who require stronger stimuli to react, are less sensitive.

The ability of a human being to adapt to their environment is going to depend in great measure on his temperament. Normally a person confronts various difficulties and adversities in his life for which he will need a certain temperament to overcome each one of those situations. Before a stressful situation, a person of strong temperament should fight to control it, since otherwise, it could bring him problems. A person with a strong temperament always has very excited or intense reactions.

Types of Temperaments

The nervous system and genes determine the type of temperament of a person. Temperament is what makes us emotionality stable, unstable; sanguine, phlegmatic, choleric, melancholy, open, extroverts, timid, or introverts.

Introversion is the tendency of a person to orientate toward his interior and have more sensibility to ideas and feelings of others. The introverts are tranquil and emotionally not too expressive. Extroversion, on the other hand, is the orientation towards other people, events, and objects. The extroverts are social, cheerful, impulsive and emotionally expressive. According to investigations, introverts handle themselves better when they are alone or in a tranquil environment, while extroverts handle themselves better in an environment with greater sensory stimuli.

People with sanguine temperaments are emotionally stable, extroverts, or open, have a varying sense of humor and have a fast but balanced nervous system. As far as people with a phlegmatic temperament, these too are emotionally stable, introverts or timid, paused, with very cold blood, and with a slow and balanced nervous system. Those people with a melancholic temperament are emotionally unstable people, introverts or timid, sad, and with a weak nervous system.

Timid people were very sensible and fearful when children, which is why they developed a tendency towards feelings of guilt and they reproach themselves. Timid children appear to be born with a network of neurons in their nervous system, which makes them sensitive even to the lightest tension. Since birth, their hearts beat faster in response to strange or new situations. They also show more anxiety and fear.

People with choleric temperaments are also emotionally unstable, extroverts or open, have a strong sense of humor and impulsive feelings. They also have a strong nervous system that is fast and a bit unbalanced. Temperament is also linked to the management of emotions and mood.

How to Modify the Temperament

Temperament, even though it comes from our genes, does not have to accompany us for life, since it can be changed with the passing of years. The emotional learning during infancy can have a profound impact over temperament, managing to modify it whether by amplifying or muffling an innate predisposition. Changing one's temperament is possible with the emotional lessons and responses that children learn as they grow. In the case of the timid child, change will depend on the way he is treated by his parents in helping him confront his natural shyness. With time, he can become a bolder child and lead a less fearful life.

It appears that the mother that overprotects a timid child does not help him come out of his shell; on the other hand, if exercises a small amount of pressure so the child can be more social, she will achieve the objective of making him bolder. One of the signs of the modification of temperament can be seen when a child overcomes his shyness and manages to develop his social skills. This suggests that emotionally innate standards can change. Likewise, a child that easily gets frightened from the time he is born can learn to be calmer and even sociable when faced with unknown things.

In summary, being timid, like any other temperamental feature, can be modified. Our environment, more than our genes, determine the way in which our temperament expresses itself as life develops, especially everything we experience and learn as we grow. This implies that our emotional capacities are not permanent and with correct learning can change for the better.

Character

From temperament sprouts character, which is a set of reactions and habits of behavior that are acquired during life and that are unique in each person. A person can have a strong or weak character. To have a strong character means to be able to respond adequately to the circumstances of life, accepting reality just as it is and developing the necessary resources to not succumb to adversity. Those who have a strong character can survive critical situations due to the firmness and solidness of their emotional structures.

People of strong character assume a firm posture with self-convictions, have dominion over themselves, and can control their impulses. They are very sure of themselves and are generally brave and always confront injustices. These people behave themselves in a sensible way and feel great respect for others. They are great fighters and they always try to help others and always offer hope.

On the other hand, people with a weak character generally before acting, consult someone to tell him or her what he or she wants to hear. They are incapable of making any important decision without the consent of someone else. They are always afraid of making decisions in order to avoid making an error and later feeling guilty. Fear and guilt are the emotions that define a weak character. One characteristic of the weak in character is the fear of losing.

Given that character is acquired, this means that it too can be modified. To strengthen his character, a person needs to learn to conquer fear since this does not permit him to take any type of risk, which is why it is so hard for him to make his own decisions to confront life with success. A person of strong character also has his fears, but confronts them and moves forward. In order to overcome fears, going to the section with the same name in subchapter 5.1 is recommended.

Temperament and character are determining factors in personality, but both can be modified. If we are not conscious of our temperament and character, these could begin directing our lives, when in reality, it should be on the contrary; we should be conscious of them and direct them in a way that will permit us to have a better life.

Self-Esteem

Self-esteem is the evaluation we make of our selves. If we consider ourselves valuable our self-esteem will be positive, but on the contrary if we feel we have little value, our self-esteem will be negative. A person with positive self-esteem feels happy with himself, which is why he has the ability to confront challenges and establish satisfactory and healthy relationships with others. He is also capable of loving and accepting himself just as he is, and he will always be willing to persevere in order to overcome challenges throughout life.

Self-esteem is of great importance to people, since what they accomplish in life will depend on their own self-value. A positive self-esteem facilitates a better perception of reality, which would help elevate our quality of life by managing uncertainty better, overcomes the processes of change, assume risks, confronts failures and frustrations as if they were opportunities to learn and grow.

People with positive self-esteem are efficient, sure of themselves, capable of confronting any situation, and in conclusion, people worthy of success. Among the characteristics of a person with adequate self-esteem are included: to appreciate and value himself, to not consider himself better or worse than what he really is, to have self-control, to have self-confidence, to express his feelings and thoughts in a free and adequate way.

People who have a negative self-esteem generally do not count on the energy necessary to confront life, loneliness affects them a lot, they do not tolerate when something does not come out as expected, are indecisive and insecure, are fearful of new situations and always need the consent of someone to make decisions.

Among other traits of people with negative self-esteem are: the inability to recognize their own capacities and abilities that make them worthy of being loved by themselves and by others. Generally, they have a self-critical attitude, are perfectionists, defeatists, not very social, and even aggressive. They always try to get attention since they have a great need to feel loved and valued. They feel great fear of being ridiculed, of being wrong, or of being a loser. They do not like to share their ideas clearly for fear of rejection.

Self-esteem begins to form during our childhood as a result of the experiences and messages inside our family and school environment that made us feel valuable and important. However, self-esteem continues its formation throughout life, which permits us as adults to make changes if necessary.

Self-esteem forms and develops progressively as the person relates with the environment. As a person acquires more knowledge about himself, he values himself more and the closer he gets to become the person he wants to be, the greater his total self-esteem will be. It is believed that the optimum point of self-esteem is when who the person is converges with what he desires to be.

In order to foster a positive concept of self-esteem, it is very important during childhood for the parents and teachers of these children to recognize and stress the positive qualities, reprove them for their errors adequately with their respective explanations without embarrassing them in front of others. They should also help them develop their abilities, express what they think, feel or belief within a frame of mutual respect.

To improve self-esteem, we should think positively according to what was discussed in point 5 of the section on management of worries in subchapter 1.4. We should also try to eradicate those negative beliefs that limit our capacities. See subchapter 4.3 on "Beliefs and Values". It is also important to be surrounded by people with positive self-esteem especially someone we admire and respect, an environment where you can hear people speak well about themselves, and where there are opportunities for achieving success.

Improving self-esteem will help us achieve pleasure, satisfaction, and self-love. That extraordinary experience will impact us with greater and better self-esteem. As confidence grow, we will put more positive energy and perseverance into the challenges and defiance of the world in which we live which will normally lead us to success, thus reinforcing our self-esteem and energy to move forward.

A Good Personality

Apart from good temperament and character, as well as positive self-esteem, personality requires some other details in order to become a good personality. A person with a good personality from the start is attractive, pleasant, and interesting, which becomes the key that will open the door to success. Everything else that happens upon crossing that threshold will depend on how a person interacts with others. This constitutes another important aspect of a good personality, the management of interpersonal relationships. Pleasant people have the ability to establish friendly interpersonal relationships. They are altruistic, considerate, confident, supportive, and have great sensitivity towards others. Attractive, pleasant, and interesting people become people others want to be with and share with.

We can manage our personality as much as we want to since nowadays; we have become aware that we have influence and control over the features and characteristics of the personality we want to develop or perfect. Of course, the easiest thing to do is to improve our physical appearance in order to be more attractive. A healthy body is vital, followed by the appropriate attire for the occasion. If the person is not very pretty, then all the more reason it is necessary to develop a good personality in order to compensate.

In order to be more pleasing, we should be friendlier and respectful with people. We must pay attention to what they say, look them in the eye, and make them feel important. It is very pleasing to have someone who listens to us with attention and makes us feel as if we were the most important person in the world. To be more interesting, we should speak of topics that are important not only to us, but to others as well. For this, we need to read more and expand our knowledge. The more well educated we are, the more interesting we will be to others.

By meeting new people, we will have the opportunity to share what we know and exchange points of view. In a conversation, we should always try to give our opinion when it is called for. And when it is called for, we should express it freely. It can be very boring to speak with someone who has no opinion about anything or that is trying to be who he really isn't. Remember that each one of us should be unique. If we are shy, we should try to discuss topics we know most about in order to become more confident.

Meeting new people expands our horizons as we find out about other ways of seeing the world, different cultures, and alternative ways of doing things. It is clear that throughout our lives we meet many people, but we always prefer to be and share with those people with whom we have most in common with.

Another important aspect of our personality is our way of thinking. If we think positively, we are known as positive people. Negative people complain all the time and generally do not have anything good to say, therefore, they are less desirable to be around. In fact, the majority of people avoid negative people. On the other hand, people should be positive and should radiate their energy wherever they go, so that they may share this light with others.

A good personality will be carried out by the values of a human being. These include: honesty, respect, and responsibility, like we will see ahead in detail in the section "Values" of subchapter 4.3. Honest, respectable, and responsible people are very attached to the truth, order, and justice. They also have a high sense of obligation with self-control and self-discipline. They are organizers, planners, competent, persistent, reliable, and punctual. They search for success. These people have managed to have an excellent personality and have always been very successful in each aspect of their lives. Every project they take on can be stamped with the seal of success.

Besides this, the people with a good personality should be open minded, emotionally stable, extroverted, and with a great sense of humor. It is important to be an *open minded* person, who is also willing to change their point of view if necessary when new facts are encountered. People with a closed mind try to resist to any change. Open-minded people generally lead a happy life. Their imagination awakens in them the curiosity for new ideas within legal and sound customs of course. Instead, people with closed minds tend to be very conventional and always stick to the same old things.

Emotionally stable people are calm, secure, and satisfied. Emotional stability equips a person with resistance to anxiety, depression, and irritability. Emotionally unstable people are on the contrary, anxious, insecure, have lots of worry, and are characterized by being neurotic and of having a biased against negative situations. *Extroverted* people are characterized by being social, pleasant, and have the tendency to experiment positive emotions like happiness and satisfaction. They are assertive and talkative. On the opposite end, introverted people are characterized by being reserved and prefer the usual and the habitual. They also prefer to be alone rather than in any social situations that are very animated.

It is also very important for a virtuous personality to have good sense of humor, as we will see ahead concerning this topic in the section on the right attitude of this same chapter. We all like to be among people with a good sense of humor since everyone enjoys the company of someone who makes them laugh.

4.3 Beliefs and Values

Beliefs are of great importance in our lives because on them will depend the perception we will have about ourselves, and the world around us. In fact, each person's reality will depend on his beliefs. Depending on our way of thinking, beliefs can be rational if they are supported by evidence or irrational if they are not substantiated. The first type can help us survive while the second one will only put limitations on our ability to achieve things.

Beliefs will mold the lives of people converting them in time into open or closed-minded people. Open-minded people accept new ideas while closed-minded people will hold tightly to theirs beliefs as the only reality. Another great impact on the life of a person is the belief he has about his destiny. Some people believe that their destiny has already been written, while others understand that they forge their own destiny by the way they think.

Prejudices can also come out of negative beliefs with an adverse impact on people. Besides their beliefs, the other aspect of great importance in the life of a person is their values. Among the more influential ones are honesty, respect, and responsibility. People with these values enhance their chances for performing better in life.

Beliefs

Beliefs are firm feelings of certainty that we have about something or someone. These mental affirmations are considered true by the person even though they may have no logical basis. Beliefs are formed from ideas that we confirm through the things we perceive with our senses, especially the things we hear from people who are important to us; from what we live, from what we believe as good or bad, useful or useless.

When a belief is installed in a concrete way, we cling to it as our own great and unique truth, without questioning it. This is the reason why we generally are so reluctant to modify any of them. The degree of conviction of beliefs depends on the power of suggestion from where the idea came. The more power of suggestion in the information, or the person who emits it has, the greater the influence that this belief will exercise over our conduct, which generally manifests itself in an unconscious way.

Beliefs can be rational or irrational depending on our way of thinking. If we think logically, our beliefs will reflect with greater objectivity, reality, and can even be substantiated by scientific evidence. Rational beliefs can be realistic and can help us survive. For this reason, they are referred as positive. This type of belief improves our self-esteem. If on the contrary, we think in an irrational way, our beliefs will also be irrational since they are based on the interpretation of our circumstances.

Like all ideas, beliefs can be positive or negative. Rational beliefs are positive since they can be a resource that can help us achieve something, while irrational beliefs are negative since they would only put limitations in a person's ability to achieve. Good or bad, beliefs are of great importance in our life because they affect the perception we have about ourselves, about others and the world around us. In fact, the personal reality of each individual will depend on his beliefs and not in reality itself. Based on that reality, people will live their life, and their achievements will depend on it.

Positive beliefs help our confidence take root in us and in our capacity to achieve things, allowing us to confront any situation in life successfully. While negative beliefs do the opposite and what is worse, they can make us lose any important opportunity that presents itself in our life to achieve our goals and likewise, can create barriers in the development of our abilities, simply because the very existence of those talents and abilities contradict the negative beliefs. Ideally, our beliefs should help us make life easier and not limit our ability to accept other ideas that can help us improve our lives.

In order to gain a better control of our lives, we should know our beliefs, determine which ones can help and which ones can limit us, and make the necessary changes to modify or remove those problematic beliefs. If you think you are useless, you will never be any good for anything. If a person believes that life is tough, they will never have an easy life. A person that believes that money is not good will never have it. Now, there is not much we can accomplish in life without money. A person that believes that in order to have money you have to work a lot will always live to work. If you think that people of the opposite sex are bad, then you will never have a partner.

People lead their life according to their beliefs. This is why they always put into practice what they believe. Beliefs will mold the lives of the people, converting them into open or closed-minded individuals. This is an extremely important realization for people trying to achieve what they want in life.

Open and Closed Minded People

People that can accept new ideas are referred to as open minded people while those that hold on to their beliefs as the only reality and accept nothing else, are closed minded people. People should understand that their beliefs are something very personal and therefore are not universal and so to pretend that the rest of the world has to accept them is foolish. This has been the biggest mistake on the part of closed minded people for a long time, especially since they are so closed minded that they have come to develop a frenetic fanaticism over some doctrine or dogma.

Some closed minded people can become an enormous social problem when they begin to blame a society for all of their calamities. In this sense, they come to the extreme thinking that it is society that denies them the place they should be occupying in it and end up as social misfits with all the implications that this brings.

Some of them believe in God, but when irrationally seeing that God does not send them hamburgers from heaven, they lose the little faith they have and start to create a type of messianic culture. This is something that a lot of politicians take advantage of by offering them hamburgers from the government palace for their vote. After their election, these politicians fail to fulfill their promises to lessen hunger, and thus the frustration deepens. These people now faithless, and hopeless, can become antisocial and go in search of relief in drugs.

As these people continue believing that someone else, not them, is responsible for their destiny, their belief becomes more rigid and they become more closed off until they reach a high level of dogmatism. Dogmatic people have a negative point of view about society and perceive the world as something bad that needs to be changed. In this endeavor they develop an aggressive fanaticism in favor of authoritative leaderships, holding on strongly to their doctrines. These people see others that do not coincide with them as enemies, which have to be exterminated. We can see that to a closed minded person will cost a lot to achieve some happiness and even worse; if they believe their destiny has already been written.

Destiny: is it written?

Another big impact in the life of a person is the belief that he has about his destiny, which refers to the series of events that occur during his life. Some people believe in what is called written destiny. It is important to understand that these events do not happen because they were already pre-written, but because they obey our way of thinking. If we are always thinking about something good, a good event will cross our path. We are physically a collection of atoms, which make our bodies be linked to our planet and to the cosmos where we come from. However, what we do or do not accomplish with our bodies during our life is tightly linked to our thought.

It is us, the people, who are responsible for our destiny. Using our way of thinking, intelligence, and effort we can achieve a life filled with happiness. Success depends on us and if for some reason this does not happen, we should examine our thoughts. There is no one to blame. Generally people who believe their destiny is their own responsibility develop faith and hope in themselves, which gives them self-motivation.

If you believe that your destiny is written, then do not continue reading this book since nothing of what is written here can help you. People that believe that their destiny has already been written do nothing to help themselves and live their lives as it comes. If something comes out wrong, they will blame someone else for their misfortune. People who tend to think that their problems are not due to their way of being but on external factors, like luck, society or God, can tend to continually fabricate, beliefs that end up submerging them deeper into hopelessness. Some of these people can even come to say that they were born with bad luck or blame society or even God for their problems, developing a series of prejudices.

Prejudices

The other aspect of negative beliefs is prejudices. Even though these also may be formed long before and serve to stimulate negative beliefs. Whichever the case, prejudices have a great impact on people. Even when these have formed in infancy, the convictions that are used to justify them surge later on in adulthood. Prejudices can be difficult to completely eradicate depending on how open the mind of the person is.

Prejudice means to judge someone in advance or form a judgment or negative opinion of that person without knowing him or her or without an examination of the facts. The majority of the people have prejudices and at some time have also been victims of prejudice. Generally, prejudices are formed over some characteristics of an individual or group, like race, culture, socioeconomic status, religion, etc. Prejudice frequently leads to discrimination.

In order to reduce the formation of prejudices and its consequences, we should try to know the people with whom we relate. In this sense it is recommended to treat people pleasantly, with respect and harmony even when these people are different from us in terms of culture, religion, race, etc.

Values

Among the factors that greatly influence the development of a good attitude towards life are values that the person develops such as: honesty, respect, and responsibility. Honest, respectable, and responsible people have self-esteem, which increases their chances for achieving a better life.

These values are developed in people throughout their lives and tend to elevate their personality. Honesty, like respect and responsibility, are fundamental values in making living relationships and communication efficient among people. These three fundamental values are indispensable for the emergence of confidence.

Honesty constitutes one of the most important values in the formation of personality and attitude towards life since it constitutes the basis of personal relationships. It is the value that makes us consistent in what we say, think, and do, not only in our behavior with others, but also with ourselves. Honesty is the supreme value of a person since this value in itself makes the other values shine no matter how opaque they are. On the contrary, dishonesty would tarnish any other value no matter how bright it may be.

Honesty conducts us to speak in a clear and sincere way with those around us and in this way it prevents us from lying. To be honest in itself represents a guaranty of happiness. In fact, honesty can be seen not only as the highest value in a person, but also as a way of life.

It would seem that the value of honesty is understood by all however, only a few practice it. This is why is not worth it to bother asking someone if they are honest since 97% of the people would tell you yes. On the other hand, if you observe them you will see that only 3% of them are. A person is honest when he or she has experienced affirmatively a situation in which they could have taken advantage to be dishonest, but chose instead to be honest.

Respect, is the other great value that permits people to recognize, accept, appreciate and value the qualities and rights of others. Respect permits people to live in certain harmony, in a healthy coexistence on the basis of norms, rights and obligations. Respect means not doing to others what you do not want done to you.

Normally, respect always attaches itself to truth. It does not tolerate lying or deceit.

Respect is the essence of any interpersonal relationship, whether it is friendship, matrimonial, work, or business. This value in people demands pleasant and courteous treatment. It also favors security and cordiality and permits the acceptance of limitations and the recognition of virtues in others. It also avoids offenses, ironies, and violence from becoming the means to impose criteria. We all feel that we have the right to be respected by others and to act and express ourselves freely. This demands from us the obligation to equally respect other people.

As far as *responsibility*, this value is rooted in the conscious mind of a person, which permits him to reflect, administer, direct, and value the consequences of his actions, always under a moral perspective. A responsible person fulfills his obligations in a correct manner and does things, as they should be. Responsibility assumes the consequences of all those actions that we take in a free and conscious way. It is one of the most important human values, since it allows us to maintain our society in order.

Responsible people always take into consideration the intention of what they are doing and do not question nor limit them in doing basic things, but instead, do the best to fulfill their objectives. On the other hand, a person that is not responsible always looks for some excuse to justify what he did, apart from not showing any serious compromise in gritty issues

4.4 A Good Friend

To develop a good attitude in life, we should be people's friend. A good friend is someone that gives us something to drink when we are thirsty, or gives us something to eat when we are hungry, or lends us a hand when we have fallen. It is someone who tries to help us convert our weaknesses into strengths. He who learns to be a friend will be good in all his endeavors. A good friend can maintain good relationships with others, which is very positive for the growth and development of a person. Friends are free to manifest any complaint for something they don't like from the other person and even criticize the cause of the complaint. If the criticism is made with good intentions, then the criticism can be constructive. But on the contrary, if it is done to hurt the other person, the criticism is negative.

A good friend, through the art of perceiving the world, understands that not everyone identifies it in the same way which is why he knows how he sees it and how others see it to better understand them. In this way, he will have a better understanding of the world that surrounds him and develop an attitude that will allow him to work with people, for people, and through people. Another important aspect of a good friend is his capacity for forgiveness. To forgive is to remove any feelings of resentment and bitterness that an offense could have created. The inability to forgive can generate much unhappiness. This is what a good friend does when he practices the art of forgiveness.

What is a Good Friend?

The human being by nature grows and develops their ability to relate to other people, which is why we normally like to have friends and share with them. Just like our ancestors did back in that time when we had to separate ourselves from our friends and family to go find food, which could take many long days. Ah! But, after returning with food, we felt double satisfaction; one from being newly reunited, and the other, from sharing our affection as well as the food we had gotten. With the passing of time we have developed tighter ties among friends and have converted our relationships with them into something stronger.

Friendship is a relationship of reciprocated affection between two people and one of the most common interpersonal ties in human beings throughout their lives. Friendship is based on confidence, respect, cooperation, and love. This type of relationship is an exchange of feelings with another person with whom we share confidences, experiences, emotions, sufferings, joys, successes, failures, and the one to whom we give of ourselves without any interest and without expecting anything in return. True friendship is sincere and loyal.

It is very important to have and make good friendships to in order to develop the true attitude towards life. And thus, we can obtain what we want from it, our happiness. A person with difficulties in relating to others, whether it be from excessive timidity, low self-esteem or any other feeling of inferiority, or simply because he does not have the capacity to socialize, will find it very difficult to achieve something with or through people. In fact, a person that does not have consideration with others and that tends to humiliate and constantly ridicule other people will hardly be a good friend.

One of the attitudes with the most profound impact in our lives is that of being a good friend, since not only can we enter into the hearts of people and remain there for a long time, but also because it makes possible the conquering of many thing in life. It is true that there are not many good friends, so when you find one, keep them, and don't ever let them go. To offer support to others when they need it makes us loved people. Who would not love someone who gave them something to drink when they were thirsty or fed them when they were hungry or lent them a hand when they had fallen?

A friend is always beside you through the different circumstances of life. The one, who learns to be a friend, will also be a good son, good father, good husband, good worker, good role model, and a good citizen. A good friend should have a lot of love, understanding, and compassion for his neighbor, and always be ready to help them. When this affection is reciprocated, the friendship grows and revitalizes with the passing of time. A good friend transmits confidence and originates a feeling of gratitude, which will increase self-esteem and strengthen the personality.

To be a good friend you need to have a great empathetic capacity to better cooperate with the other person and try to better understand what they feel. Besides, it is fundamental to have a good personality and good communication with others, to listen to, and understand them, respect their opinions and thoughts even when they are contrary to yours, and never get upset when they contradict you. It is also essential to recognize the merits and talents of other people.

A good friend never attacks the other person for his weaknesses. On the contrary, when he sees weaknesses in others, he tries to convert them into strengths. This is basically the difference between a friend and an enemy. The friend will always be saddened by the misfortunes of others, but is happy when they are happy. A good friend will always be with the person in the most difficult moments. Just like my good friend, Mr. Antonio has told me in various occasions.

He tells me that there once was a son who would brag to his father about having many friends. However, the father felt certain doubt about the authenticity of the friendships, so eventually he convinced him to test these friends. The boy went and appeared at the house of one of his "friends", knocked on the door and told him with some nervousness and desperation to open the door because he had a problem. The "friend" opened the door, saw the boy with a bag from which a little blood was dripping and asked, "What is the matter?" to which the boy responded that he was rammed and he had to defend himself. The "friend" did not want to continue talking to him and closed the door.

Thus, he went to see three more "friends" and the story was similar. With much frustration and deception, the son looked at his father and the father asked him for the bag. The father carried the bag to see a friend of his. He arrived at the house of the friend and knocked on the door. When the friend opened the door, he asked, "What is the matter?" The father of the boy responded the same as his son had done with his friends. The father's friend told him, "Come in quickly because we must resolve this problem now."

A good reward will always await a good friend. The friend of the boy's father after having opened the bag and sees that what was inside was a deer, asked the boy's father..." but what is the matter?" To which the boy's father responded, "This deer rammed me while I was hunting, and in order to defend myself I had to kill him. I have brought it here because I wanted to share it with my best friend and my son. Thank you for being my friend!"

The Relationships with Others

A good friend can maintain healthy relationships with others and have a true friend, which is very positive to grow and develop as a person. Sound management of our interpersonal relationships has enormous benefits; it increases our ability to analyze and comprehend relationships, makes us considerate with others, and helps us develop better communication skills, which helps us resolve conflict and other problems in our relationships.

The most important thing in all relationships is to know how to handle difficulties when they present themselves. Any displeasure if not attended to on time and in an adequate way can put the relationship at risk to the point of dissolution. Reaching this point could be considered a consequence of bad management of emotions. If they are not controlled, these emotions will overflow reducing the capacity of the person to think clearly which could induce him to say or do something that would accelerate the breakup of the relationship.

Of course, in a friendship circle, if friends can decide to end the relationship for whatever reason, whenever they want to and simply everything ends. However, ending a marital relationship can be much more complex. Once a friend told me that he wanted to see me because he wanted to divorce his wife. He told me he was tired of his wife and that they lived offending each other in constant arguments, which at times were so heated up that they would end in fights.

For a relationship to function it is necessary to not concentrate on recurring discussions but to learn to better manage and control their emotions. The simple act of listening to one another can make it more probable for the disagreements to dissipate more successfully. Another good strategy in a time of a heated discussion is to calm down so that the ability to listen, think and talk can regain its clarity.

The point is that at the request of this friend, I went to his house to meet his wife and I stayed three days with them to see how their relationship was. This friend had a bad temper and his emotions would overflow easily so that the emotional assault would not take long to appear. She also had a similar temperament but not as bad as him. Both of them were already almost 50 years old and had been married for more than 20 years and had two children.

After listening to them and observing them, I recommended to my friend not to get divorced. To which he said, "It seems you don't understand me." I really did understand him and I told him that as his good friend I was telling him what I considered good for him and not simply what he wanted to hear. I asked him, "What are you going to do if you get divorced?" He told me he would remarry. With what I knew about him, it was sufficient to predict that it would cost him a lot to find another wife due to his personality, his low capacity of making friends, his age, and his scarce physical attraction.

I told him that in this life there was time for everything including marriage and divorce, but for him that time had passed. If he divorced, more than likely they both would end up alone; a life that would be difficult to lead. However, if he did find someone, there was no guarantee that it would work due to his temperament. Now, that uncertainty would disappear if he stayed with his wife since she at least kept tolerating him. Besides, there were two children with certain emotional problems, as a product of perhaps their parents' situation. Staying together could help the two kids.

At the end of my second day with them, my friend comes up to me and tells me that he had been thinking about all I had said, but he felt she no longer was very interested in him since she didn't look for him. "Why would she have to look for you?" I told him; "Perhaps she is thinking the same thing about you." The truth is that when I was saying goodbye to my friends, he hugged his wife and it seemed that they headed to their bedroom. Later, I would see them in the celebration of their 27th wedding anniversary.

Respect and love are considered the key to success in any type of relationship. However, when relationships start to have problems, it is also very important that even when a person is not a good friend, for whatever reason, he should always have by his side a friend to help him through difficult times. A good friend can always see things from another perspective. Another very important aspect in keeping a good relationship and that a friend can manage well, is the criticism towards other people.

Fair Criticism

In a healthy relationship, friends are free to voice any complaint concerning something that displeases them about the other person, even to criticize the cause of the complaint. If the criticism is done with the intention to improve that which is being criticized, then the criticism can be constructive or positive. If on the contrary, it were done to hurt or anger the other person, the criticism would be destructive or negative. Only positive criticism, such as love, builds, while negative ones destroy, such as hate.

Now when criticism is frequent, to the point of reaching a heated discussion, the criticism turns rough, becoming a personal attack on the other person and takes on a destructive form. This could be a sign that the relationship is deteriorating. A criticism can be positive or negative depending on the intention with which it is made, the words, and the way they are said, and even more importantly, on how it is interpreted by the person who receives it.

Negative criticism makes the person who receives it feel ashamed, reproached, and disgusted. All this, far from improving anything, worsens things; especially when the criticism is full of contempt, which tends to be expressed not only in words, but also in a tone of anger. Its most evident form is mockery, insult, or reproach. Just as damaging is the corporal language that expresses contempt, especially the mocking smile. A good friend is always careful to manage criticism.

To avoid misunderstandings and not make criticism a problem, this should be done over something very specific. Present the problem and its possible solution in front of the criticized person, but never behind their back. A positive or constructive criticism can be a powerful tool in the sense that it can help us make the adjustments that a relationship needs to improve its functioning.

It is also important that criticism is done timely to correct the problem and not wait until things are out of control, or the person cannot contain his anger and starts to express the criticism in the worst way, with a bitter tone, full of sarcasm and remembering a list of complaints that had been kept quiet.

The Art of Perceiving the World

A good friend understands that not all of us perceive the world the same way, which is why he should understand how he sees it and how others see it to better understand them. In this way, we will have a better understanding of people and the world that surrounds us in order to develop an attitude that will permit us to work with people, for people and through people.

For example, the reason why the majority of the people leave their jobs is because of problems communicating with their boss. Since, believing that their way of perceiving the world is not compatible with their boss', they leave their job and that's it. But what would happen if the person whom he cannot understand happens to be his wife? Would he leave her and that's it? It is here where we see very well the importance of understanding the perception that others have of other people, to understand them and coexist with them.

All people think differently and each one looks at the world under his own perspective or unique way of perceiving it. The majority of people, almost always perceive the world in one way but the worst thing is that they come to believe that that is the only correct way of doing it. This precisely has been the problem of understanding among people due to the fact that many other ways of perceiving the world really do exist and they are different and even opposite of ours.

Our way of perceiving the world is important because it dictates our focus towards other people, problems and in great measure, our general behavior. It is also important to understand how other people perceive the world. From this understanding will depend the success of people in their relationships to others since through this comprehension, people can have the appropriate orientation in order to find the solution to any difficult situation with other people.

Very few people perceive the world, or focus on a situation in more than two ways. Half of the people tend to perceive the world in one way while the other 35% do it in a combination of more than two ways. In reality, and according to experts, there exist 5 different ways for perceiving the world which people learn as they grow. Each one of these ways of perception has its strong and weak points. We should try to understand and respect how other people perceive the world to make coexisting with them possible. These different ways of perceiving the world are the: synthesist, idealist, realist, pragmatist, and analyst.

The Synthesist

Synthesists are very speculative and are always asking themselves; what would happen if...? These people never agree on anything and are very contradictory and conflicting. If they ever reach an agreement, it would not last more than 7 minutes before they changed their minds. Synthesists are fascinated when they hear from politicians the word change. They always vote for them.

The Idealist

Idealists are people that like to have a wide vision of things. Their constant question is; where are we going and why? This is why they are interested by the needs of people and social values. Idealists like to be seen by other people as trustworthy and useful people that help and support. They tend to have a strong sense of ethics. They see themselves as good people, who do the right thing, and that they will have their just reward.

Idealists also tend to be particularly interested in the quality of life and what is good for people and for society in conjunction. When it comes to solving problems, the best situation for an idealist would be in the important things like values, judgments, feelings, and emotions.

The Pragmatist

For the pragmatist, anything that works is fine with him, even though he is always looking for new ways to do things with the resources at his disposal. Actions and values weigh the same for them and emotions and feelings will become actions only if they are relevant to the situation. The people who perceive the world in this way tend to focus on problems in a gradual way, in other words, one thing at a time. Perhaps because of this, to other people, it could appear that their focus is superficial.

Pragmatists tend to be less predictable than people with other ways of perceiving the world. They always try to be likable, they like to socialize and be jovial. They love the negotiation involved in buying and selling, bargaining or asking for a lower price, and to have quick rewards. They are flexible and adaptable. Pragmatists do not have much interest in a global vision of things like idealists, nor in the logical and planned focus of the analyst.

The Analyst

The analyst perceives the world logically, rationally, orderly, and predictably. These people treat problems in a very careful way, logically, methodically, paying very close attention to details until the problem is resolved. They try to always comprehend all the facets of any situation in which they find themselves. They are great planners and always have a theory about almost everything. They analyze and judge things in a wide margin that helps explain things and reach conclusions.

The focus of analysts is very different from the other ways of perceiving the world. While synthesists hold on to conflicts, change and novelty; the analyst prefers rationalism, stability and predictability. While the idealist centers on values, goals, and the global panorama; the analyst prefers to concentrate on the objective facts, procedures, and the best method. If the focus of the pragmatist is fragmented and experimental, in the analyst, on the contrary, it is planned and based on the search for a better way.

The Realist

Realists focus on real things, in other words, in what they can perceive with their senses. You can always hear them say that facts are facts. The realist is contrary to the synthesist in the sense that for the synthesists deductions are more important than facts. In the other hand, while the synthesist is firmly convinced that agreement and consensus is not very probable to happen among people, the realist believes that agreement and consensus are very important.

Realists like to fix things and are oriented towards achieving concrete results. In this sense they are like the analysts, since both believe in actions and are oriented towards the objective, and the concrete. However, the realist is impatient with the long procedures of the analyst. The realist is inductive and practical, while the analyst is deductive and analytical.

Of course there is no one who perceives the world completely in only one of these ways or styles. The perception of people is always a combination of these forms. But, there will always be a tendency to perceive the world in one of these ways. The important thing is to have this knowledge and to try to analyze people with whom we interact to achieve the best out of our relationships, treating them according to their perception of the world.

For example, if we want to have a good relationship with a synthesist we should not include extensive analytical explanations in our interaction with him, since he will not be interested. In fact, synthesis is the opposite of analysis. Neither should we give him a compass of options because we will confuse him. The synthesist responds better when he is told in a direct way what he has to do. Likewise, if we want to have a good relationship with a realist, we have to go to the main point so he can consider our point of view. The best way to have a good understanding with a pragmatist is using a good sense of humor. While, the best way to understand an idealist is to simply speak with your heart in your hand.

It is of high importance to know how people perceive the world in which we interact. With practice and experience, we can place the perception of people after hearing them for the first 7 minutes of the conversation. Once we know whom we are dealing with, we will direct the conversation according to what we want to achieve, whether it be flirting or selling something.

The Art of Forgiving

Forgiving is a practice that many times carries with it a feeling of relief for the forgiver as well as for the forgiven. To the one who forgives, it allows him to get out of his soul any feeling of resentment or bitterness that an offense could have created. To the forgiven, it also makes him feel better, allowing him to remove a bit of the feeling of guilt that could have originated from the offense. For the relationship of the offended and the offender forgiveness could help restore the break in the relationship due to the offense.

Now, to forgive does not mean that things between the people involved will continue on the same course that it had before the offense. Forgiveness simply removes the perturbing feelings that cause us pain as a result of the offensive situation. I remember a friend that had a friendship with another friend for more than 27 years until one day the friend offended him because of a political issue. That person was his best friend, almost a brother, whom he had helped a lot from the moment he met him. After the incident, the tear in the friendship became so vast that it ended up fracturing the relationship.

These two friends were never again the same. About 7 months after the incident, the offender called the offended and told him that it seemed like he had not forgiven him. The offended replied; "Yes, I really have forgiven you, only that forgiveness is not how the majority of the people take it." How can it be that someone can offend someone else and later tell him he's sorry and that's it? It is not that simple. It is because of this that we speak here about the art of forgiveness.

It is understood that to err is human and that any person can, even without meaning to offend another person, especially at the beginning of the relationship. But in a relationship of almost a lifetime, an offense is almost unacceptable, since it is assumed that throughout that relationship the people have had all the sufficient time in the world to get to know each other better unless, one of them or both has not been honest with the other.

If we do not practice forgiveness, all the suffering that it causes us when we are offended or hurt by others, could turn to resentment which is a feeling of hostility against those that have offended us and if we do not know how to manage it and we let that negative feeling overtake us, we could be producing a lot of emotional as well as, physical damage. Definitely, by the experiences of each one of us, we can see that the inability to forgive generates much unhappiness, which is what a good friend tries to avoid by practicing the art of forgiveness.

Now, how do we know that we truly have forgiven someone? Simple, if someone were to tell us something good about someone that offended us and it causes us discomfort, then that attitude signifies that the seeds of resentment are still active in our mind and that the forgiveness, if there was one, was not sincere. But on the contrary, if we could assume a calm attitude without feeling any displeasure by the good things we hear about this person, then we can really say that the forgiveness was sincerely executed.

4.5 The Right Attitude

Attitude is a person's learned way of acting towards life. When our way of acting helps us reach what we want or confront with success any situation that presents itself, we say that our attitude is right or positive. A person with the right attitude concentrates on making use of his resources to solve his problems instead of worrying about the resources he doesn't have. In other words, these people do not allow the things they cannot do to stop them from doing what they can. To have the right attitude in life is like being a magnet attracting all the things it desires.

In order to develop the right attitude, besides having developed a good personality, positive beliefs and good values, and becoming a good friend, we should also be optimistic, have faith and hope, have a positive attitude towards, money, have a good sense of humor, and be free from vices. Optimism helps people confront the adversities of life and leads them to go on despite the obstacles in the way until success is reached. People that have faith and hope have more possibility of achieving the objectives in their life. We should develop a positive attitude towards money in order to have it. This attitude consists in believing in money, wanting to have it, and using it to do right. People with a good sense of humor generate more positive thoughts, which help them resolve problems that appear in the path towards a better life. To a person with a vice, especially if he consumes illegal drugs, it will be very hard to achieve the right attitude in life, since the vices will try to halt his intent. It is extremely necessary that people are free from vices in order to achieve a full life.

Optimism

Being optimistic means to have great expectations things will turn out right in life, despite mishaps and frustrations. Optimism is an attitude that prevents people from falling into apathy, hopelessness, or depression in the face of adversity. Just like hope, optimism offers many benefits in life, as long as the optimism is balance and realistic, since an optimism that is far from reality can result in not being very healthy.

Optimistic people consider failure as a postponement of victory, which in the next opportunity can lead to success. While the pessimists immediately assume guilt for over a failure, trying to justify it with any excuse, and consider themselves as failures. Optimism has profound implications in the way people react when confronted with the adversities in life, which normally lead a person to success. Successful people have the

combination of reasonable talent and the ability to
continue forward despite the obstacles in the way, thanks
to hope and optimism.

Optimism also produces the sufficient motivation
to continue forward despite adverse situations. Optimists
see the world in a different way. They are sociable and
happy, they experience sensations of delight, often are in
good humor, have a marked security in themselves, and
feel gratified by life. They also have fewer propensities
for depression and other emotional disorders.

The good news for pessimists is that optimism and
hope can be learned (I hope they don't say no). For this, it
is important to believe that one is self-sufficient, has
dominion over the events of his life, and can accept
challenges just as they present themselves. An optimistic
attitude makes people have more probabilities of utilizing
their abilities in an optimal way, or to do the necessary
thing to develop them. People that have an idea of self-
sufficiency recuperate from failures and address things to
manage them instead of worrying about what could go
bad.

Faith and Hope

Two attitudes exist which we should pay close attention
to, since they are indispensable for achieving any thing in
life even happiness itself. Without them, reaching what
we want would result in a steep climb. In the case where
we already possess these traits we will have great part of

the goal resolved. Otherwise, we should cultivate them immediately. These two great attitudes are faith and hope.

In general - people who have faith and hope - have more possibility of achieving their objective since these two attitudes together play an important role in achieving everything we want. Faith is the energy that helps us reach our goals, while hope is believing that one has the will and also the means to reach their objectives whatever they may be.

People that show higher levels of faith and hope, are capable of self-motivation, of feeling sufficiently able to achieve their goals, and of thinking when they are in a bind, that things will get better. To have faith and hope helps us not to be overwhelmed by anxiety and not have an attitude of defeat when confronting challenges and mishaps. In effect, people that have faith and hope have less emotional difficulties. To have faith and hope is to be optimistic.

Attitude towards Money

It would be extremely difficult, if not impossible, to perceive today's world without money. This perhaps, may not be everything in life, but it almost is. We need it for everything, to the point that there is no aspect in our lives in which it is not necessary. But, in order to have it, we must develop the right attitude towards it. This attitude is nothing more than to believe in money, want to have it, and to use it for good.

In life, we will only attract the things, which we identify with and the things, which we have a positive attitude towards. Money is one of those things that nobody will be able to have unless they feel love for it, in order to take it and multiply it so people can be productive. Just as it is written in the parable of the Ten Minas in the Holy Scriptures.

In the Gospel of Luke chapter 19, verses 11-27; the parable of the Ten Minas, Jesus taught this parable on his way to Jerusalem, a little before his triumphant entrance into this city. The parable tells the story of a nobleman who left to a faraway country to receive a kingdom and then return. He called ten of his servants and gave them ten minas, one for each one of them. He then said to them: "Manage until I come. Make the best use of this money". Upon his return, after having received the kingdom, he called those servants to whom he had given the money to come before him to see what each one had produced. The first one came saying: "Master, your mina has gained ten minas". He said to him: "Well done, good servant; you have been faithful in little; you will have authority over ten cities". The faithfulness of the servant was greatly rewarded. Then came another, saying: "Master, your mina has produced five more minas." The master also said to him: "You too will have authority over five cities". The diligence in the service is never in vain. The other simply said: "Master, here is the mina you gave me, which I have kept, in a handkerchief because I was afraid". The nobleman, very angry took it away from him for having been negligent in his obligations and gave it to the one who had gained 10 minas for having recognized his obligations and having fulfilled them. An objection presented itself among those present listening, which was answered by the master. Notice what the master replied to their objection. They said: "Master, he already has ten minas" and the master replied: "I say unto you, everyone who has, more shall be given; but from him that has not, even what he has shall be taken away from him".

The parable could not be any clearer, just like its interpretation; money attracts money since the one who has the most will have more. There is no doubt that God wants us to be prosperous. That is the essence of the parable of the ten minas. Many people believe that being poor looks good before the eyes of God. We can see it is not so. Poverty is only a mental condition. God wants us to be productive and for this we must make very effective use of our money. To obtain it, it is necessary to have a positive attitude toward money so it can always be with us for our good and the good of our families and friends. The money we obtain in life should always be used to do good.

Good Sense of Humor

Humor is a mood or emotional disposition that a person has in a determined moment when is confronted with events in life and that manifests itself exteriorly in a determined attitude whether it is with happiness or sadness. The state of mind or mood that surges as a result of an emotion or feeling, determines the humor of the person, his way of thinking, and seeing the world. When people are in a good humor or happy, they will generate more positive thoughts making it easier to find solutions to their problems. A good sense of humor helps us manage and control our emotions.

A person with good humor laughs which brings him great benefits. Laughter helps people think with greater broadness and clarity. People that are in good humor are more perceptive, communicative, and positive. Likewise, to be in a bad humor, leads to negative directions, resulting in making it more probable to adopt a fearful excessively careful decision.

Sense of humor is the capacity to see and stimulate the funny and entertaining side of things, other people and us. This helps respond with a positive attitude when confronted with challenges or difficult situations that we encounter in everyday life, as well as, facilitates the communication with other people. Sense of humor permits us to see life from another perspective. It makes us more relaxed and favorable to make decisions in the solution of conflicts and helps us overcome stress. Also, sense of humor is a good antidote against fear, thus when we laugh at things that scare us, they become less threatening.

A good sense of humor permits us to liberate our tensions, dissipate our worries, relax, and laugh. Laughter can be a healing tool since a good laugh strengthens the immune system of the body and reduces the hormones that can cause stress. Laughter provokes an enormous release of endorphins known as the happy hormones. Besides, with laughter we release serotonin and dopamine, which produce sensations of wellbeing. The explosion of laughter gives vitality, energy, and increases the cerebral activity. When laughter invades us, many muscles in our body that remain inactive, begin to function. It is an efficient stimulus against stress, depression, and evidently, sadness.

Free of Vices

In order to develop the right attitude in life, people should be free of bad habits or vices. A habit is anything that we do automatically and unconsciously, which can be good or bad. Vices are bad habits that are very difficult to change or eliminate. Among the causes that lead people to acquire a certain vice are; their little or non-existent self-will, a weak character, ignorance, and lack of intellectual preparation. A vice is any excessive attachment to something we must combat, especially if it is harmful to the person, family, and society. Among the most common vices in today's world are drugs and gambling.

Drugs

The use of drugs is as old as humanity. Besides its medicinal uses, in the ancient world, especially in Asia, the stimulating and pleasant effects of drugs were discovered and began to be utilized with that purpose. Today, a drug is defined as all substances that when introduced into the organism, alter the state of mind, perception, state of consciousness, mental functions, and conduct. Drugs that cause an addiction are known as stupefactions or narcotics, which cause the individual to enter into a state of sleepiness, lack of sensibility, dizziness, loss of conscious, and sleep. An addiction is the urgent need to consume drugs constantly without being able to exercise any control over the consumption much less be able to suppress it. Today in our society some legal and illegal drugs exist.

Legal Drugs

Among the most important legal drugs in our society are alcohol and tobacco. With the damage that these produce, why would we want to go in search of others? It is not understood either how even governments that supposedly are there to protect people, can promote the idea of legalizing drugs that until now have been in the black list.

Alcohol. Since ancient times, man has learned to ferment grains and juices to obtain a substance that would cause an altered mental state. The use of beer, wines, and other alcoholic beverages date back to 3,000 years before Christ, even though, the process of distillation of fermented beverages goes back to the year 800 after Christ. This process has permitted the preparation of very strong liquors whose use has brought many problems to people, family, and society in general. However, if it is done in moderation and in the permitted guidelines, alcohol can reduce tension, disinhibit and provoke sensations of well-being.

The immoderate use of alcohol produces serious damage. Alcohol is one of the drugs that has become a true social problem in almost the entire world within people of any sex and age after adolescence. The havocs of alcohol can be very serious and many of them are irreversible. When alcohol is consumed in excess and almost every day, the person can become an alcoholic. Alcoholism is characterized by a strong dependency on this drug, which produces progressive damage in the brain.

The effect of alcohol last until all of the substance has been processed, which normally lasts in a person with a weight of 165 lbs. one hour and a half for every 12oz. can of beer or 5 oz. cup of wine. The absorption of alcohol by the organism is basically determined by its concentration and the presence of food in the stomach. Of course, the body type and the sex of the person also influence. The more the person weighs, the less his absorption of alcohol will be. Generally, men are less susceptible than women. Another important factor in the absorption of alcohol is how alcoholic the person is. Advanced stages of alcoholism reduce the tolerance to alcohol.

When the concentration of alcohol exceeds certain levels in the blood, it interferes with the mental processes so that visual perception is distorted; motor coordination, balance, language, and vision also suffer strong deterioration. It is also true that strong quantities of alcohol reduce pains and physical discomforts and induce sleep. The bad thing is that the continuous use of it irritates the walls of the stomach causing ulcers to develop. Additionally, those who consume alcohol heavily and consistently tend to accumulate fat in the liver which interferes with its functioning.

The way we live today, we can have up to 3 drinks to socialize, enjoy ourselves a bit, and have a good time; always with moderation and never to get drunk. As a rule, the person should never drink on an empty stomach and should always "eat something" while he drinks. Another important aspect to avoid getting drunk is to drink slowly. Try to finish your drink in about 45 minutes to allow your body time to process it. If your drink has ice in it, like whiskey, always try to finish the drink to the same rhythm of the ice. If you drank the whiskey and there is still ice in the glass, then you are drinking too fast.

Tobacco. The tobacco plant originated in America. Indigenous people took the plant dried leaves and would put them in a pipe and as they burned, they would inhale the smoke through the pipe. When the first Europeans arrived to the American continent, they observed this totally new habit. They became interested in the practice of smoking, introduced it in Europe around the XVI century and later it progressively extended to the rest of the world. Tobacco is smoked in a pipe or cigar, but the most common form of smoking it is in a cigarette. Generally, people are initiated into the vice of smoking during the adolescence years, whether as an act of rebellion or to not feel left out of the group if this group is primarily composed of smokers. Another possibility is that the young smoke to feel like an adult.

Smoking can result in a chronic intoxication known as tabaquism or a nicotine addiction. When smoke is inhaled, the nicotine deeply penetrates the lungs from where it rapidly passes to the bloodstream and is transported to the entire body. Nicotine is a drug with a highly addictive power that is found in natural form in tobacco and affects many parts of the body, including the heart and the blood vessels, hormones, the metabolism, and the brain. Nicotine attacks vitamin C, which is responsible for the production of collagen, which maintains our tissues together. For every cigarette that people smoke, they will be destroying 25 mg of vitamin C, the equivalent of an orange. To compensate for this loss, smokers should consume more foods rich in vitamin C or take supplements in the form of pills.

To free their bodies from the addiction of nicotine, people should stop smoking. This is not an easy thing to do since the symptoms of withdrawal can be immensely unpleasant. The symptoms of abstinence can last from a few days to various weeks and will alleviate each day the person goes without smoking. Among these symptoms we can include: dizziness, depression, frustration, impatience, anxiety, irritability, sleep disorders, concentrating difficulties, headaches, tiredness, increase in appetite, weight gain, etc. These symptoms can cause the person to start smoking again in order to recuperate the levels of nicotine in the blood.

One of the easiest ways to stop this vice is to try to find some pleasure in the act of smoking. For this, it is necessary to smoke and be conscious that you are smoking. The majority of smokers smoke without realizing what they are doing and this is why they end up smoking one cigarette after another. In fact, they sometimes light up the next cigarette without having finished the one they are smoking. In order to be conscious that you are smoking, the person should try to concentrates only on smoking. Once concentrated, try to find some pleasure in the act of smoking. You will see that you will not find it. There simply isn't one.

By consuming alcohol, for example, people become happy and up to a certain point can feel better, but in the case of cigarettes, it is not the same. Not one benefit exists that comes from cigarettes. The only thing that you get from this vice, apart from ruining your health, is bad breath. Besides, no one likes to kiss an ashtray. By not feeling any pleasure in smoking, a person starts to think about how ridiculous and irresponsible this vice is. This is what this method is all about. It is a strategy against the vice in which you try to mentally ridicule the act of smoking. When this purpose has been achieved, then the rest of the task will be easier.

Now, you can start to reduce the quantity of cigarettes that are smoked per day. Of course, first you will try to eliminate those cigarettes that are smoked in between the cigarettes that are considered critical, like the one in the morning after coffee, the one after your meals, and the one before going to sleep. Afterwards, try to eliminate the less critical cigarettes until you have finished all of them. It is recommended not to drink coffee or consume alcohol while you are trying to quit smoking since these other vices make the process more difficult, especially with alcohol since when the person gets drunk, he cannot control his will.

The worst days in the process of quitting smoking are the first three days. During this time, people use all their will power to control the impulses to continue with the vice. From the fifth day on, the anxiousness to smoke is less intense and easier to overcome. It is recommended to drink water and to breathe deeper to calm the nerves. Vitamin B complex can also be a good help.

Illegal Drugs

The most consumed illegal drug in the world is marijuana, according to a report from the United Nations. Other illegal drugs of great importance for the damage they cause are opium and its derivatives and also cocaine.

Marijuana. It is a drug that comes from a plant called cannabis, which originated in Asia and expanded throughout the world. It is mainly known as hemp or Indian hemp. The Spaniards introduced the plant in America via Mexico, where cannabis acquired its name of marijuana. Later, it passed into the United States and the rest of the continent.

Marijuana is the most popular narcotic in the world. It is derived from the dried flowers of the plant and commonly is smoked like a cigarette or utilizing a pipe. The effects of the drug makes the person feel moderately inebriated, his power of concentration becomes hindered, he loses the concept of time and distances, and the colors appear more vivid and voices are heard louder.

The extreme consumption of this drug cause lethargy and lessens the mental faculties, confusion is produced, and the will to be active is lost. The consequences of the use of marijuana include memory problems, learning problems, loss of coordination, an increase in cardiac rhythm, and panic.

Opium and its Derivatives. Opium is a drug that is obtained from a plant called somniferum whose use has extended throughout the world. The generic name of somniferum is papaver. However, when the Spaniards introduced the plant in Mexico, it was given the name amapola (poppy). From the amapola fruit, opium and its derivatives are derived. Its principal component is morphine, which possesses all the pharmaceutical properties from which derive many other compounds like heroine.

Opiates or opium derivatives produce addiction and dependency. Its psychological effects are similar to those of other stimulants: euphoria, energy, pleasure, and sexual vigor. However, once the effects of the drug lessen, anguish, depression, weariness, and grief appear. The prolonged consumption of this drug can produce a decline in respiratory function, a loss of reflexes, hypotension, cardiac deceleration, convulsions and risk of death.

Morphine is a drug similar to concentrated opium that is named in honor of Morpheus, the Greek God of sleep. The drug is a substance in the form of a white crystalline powder, odorless and soluble in water and is used as an analgesic to alleviate pain. Its secondary effects are depression of the respiratory, circulatory and digestive systems. Morphine is taken intramuscularly, through nasal inhalation, or by means of suppositories.

Heroin is a narcotic of the opiate family that is obtained as a derivative of morphine and is sold in the form of a white or brown powder, as well as, in the form of a black sticky substance. This drug can be sniffed, injected, or smoked to feel a sense of euphoria. Injecting it puts people at risk for contracting AIDS or hepatitis. An overdose of this drug can cause death.

Cocaine. It is a drug that is obtained from the leaves of the cocoa plant, which is a native to the high mountain ranges in South America in Bolivia, Peru, and Ecuador. The natives from that region used the cocoa leaves as a stimulant to increase breathing which in turn increased the intake of oxygen and thus compensated for the lack of it at that great altitude. From South America, the Spaniards took cocoa to Europe to use it as an anesthetic and nerve tonic.

From cocaine and through chemical processes, new methods to maximize the euphoric effects of the drug were invented which resulted in the most potent and addictive drug known as crack; a form of cocaine that has been processed to make it into a rock crystal that when heated generates vapors that are smoked. The term "crack" refers to the crackle that the rock produces when it is hot.

Cocaine is an extremely addictive stimulant that directly affects the central nervous system. The drug can be used orally, nasally, or intravenously. Generally, its effects make the user feel euphoric and full of energy, but it also increases the body temperature, blood pressure and cardiac frequency. People who consume cocaine run the risk of having a heart attack or stroke, respiratory insufficiency, convulsions, abdominal pain, and nausea.

Other Drugs. Among other drugs, we have amphetamines, ecstasy, and LSD, all with lethal effects to the people that consume them. Amphetamines are synthetic drugs that stimulate the central nervous system. They come in the form of pills or capsules of different shapes and colors. This drug produces sensations of alertness, confidence and security, increases the levels of energy and self-esteem. Besides this, it makes the sensation of hunger and sleep disappears. The use of this drug has expanded to almost all the sports due to the fact that it diminishes the sensation of fatigue. Another one of its applications, perhaps the most usual one, is the reduction of weight.

Amphetamines can be legal if taken under strict medical supervision, however, the abuse of these is produced when taken and consumed in an illegal way. Due to the increase of the consumption and business of these substances, they began to be manufactured in illegal laboratories to avoid their control, which implies a great risk, since the chemical products utilized in its manufacture are highly toxic. The long term use of amphetamines produce a very aggressive conduct with physical complications like harm to the heart, stroke, and intense fevers that can threaten life.

Ecstasy is another synthetic drug that possesses stimulant properties and hallucinogens. This drug tends to circulate in the form of tablets, pills, capsules, or powder. The majority of them contain a mixture of amphetamines, hallucinogens, and other substitutes. Generally, it is consumed orally, even though it can be injected or inhaled. Ecstasy can increase the levels of rapport by producing sensations of intimacy affective with those around them.

Among the risks associated with its consumption are: tachycardia, tremors, hallucinations, convulsions, and nausea. The most severe reaction is hyperthermia or high temperature. The habitual consumption of this drug can produce depression, disorientation, insomnia, panic attacks, and anxiety. It can also produce harm to the internal organs like the liver and kidneys, as well as, harm to certain areas of the brain, which can provoke severe depression and loss of memory.

LSD is one of the most potent drugs for changing your mood or state of mind. This chemical substance is manufactured from lysergic acid, which is found in ergot, a fungus that grows in rye and other grains. In illegal laboratories, it is produced in the form of crystals, which convert into an odorless and colorless liquid with a light bitter taste in order to distribute it. LSD is sold on the streets in small tablets; capsules or gel squares and even in liquid form. The effects that a person experiences when using LSD are described as a "trip" because of the sensation of transferring to another place-space-time.

LSD is so strong that whoever consumes it totally disconnects from reality. The use of LSD can produce serious mental alterations like states of paranoia, hallucinations, schizophrenia, anxiety, or extreme panic attacks. The frequent use of LSD produces drastic changes in the personality of the individual that negatively influence his development.

Drugs as a Social Problem

Drugs constitute an important social problem due to the negative impact they generate in people, as well as in society. In the people who consume them, drugs produce a great dependency and addiction, creating the need to consume them constantly in order to avoid the convulsive effects that appear when their use is suspended. In this way, these people dehumanize themselves and become slaves to the drug.

Apart from this, the effects of drugs on the health of people who consume them are devastating. These people end up losing their humanity and when this happens basically nothing matters to them anymore and they can end up becoming delinquents, murderers, etc. which represents an enormous problem for society. It is sad to think that all this damage is caused by groups of people, which obtain gigantic benefits.

Drugs are one of the businesses that move the highest volume of money worldwide. It produces sufficient money to buy whatever or whomever they want. They even place their own presidents in interest countries. They have sufficient power to prevent anybody from thinking they can resolve this immense problem for humanity.

It is extremely disconcerting to see how the consumption of drugs has incremented in such an abysmal way among the youth. This is very dangerous since drugs destroy the quality of a society converting it into a society full of perturbed, incapable, and sick people. Of course, a decomposed society is headed towards its own disappearance. Since if what is destroyed is the youth, what will be its generation of change? The problem with drugs is evident. Now, how can it be that being such an important problem for the survival of society, no one wants to find a solution?

Up to now we have seen that there is no political willingness to do it, which makes us think, for whatever reasons, our current governors have turned their back on their people one more time. It seems that governments are only interested in avoiding social disgust due to the consumption of drugs, because they are concerned in loosing votes instead of combating the roots of the problem to find a definitive solution.

We have heard of very important leaders in the world talking about legalizing illegal drugs as if this were the only possible solution to the problem and the worse thing is that those same politicians say that they love the people very much. How can this be true? It appears that those politicians do not care about the immense harm that drugs produce in people. They even reach the allegation that their legalization would produce more taxes for the government. Evidently, government only thinks about the benefits that these drugs could leave behind.

Drugs take the life of more than 200 thousand people each year; they produce devastation in families and cause suffering to thousands of people. Illicit drugs undermine the economic and social development and foment delinquency, instability, insecurity, and the propagation of deadly diseases like AIDS. The consumption of drugs also represent an immense financial burden for society of more than 250 million dollars which means more than a 0.3 % of the gross domestic product (GSP) worldwide to cover all the costs for the treatments related to the use of drugs in the world. Besides this, the consumption of drugs diminishes the productivity of society in approximately 0.5% of the GSP worldwide.

In regards to the drug problem, like in many others, people have remained alone. Only us, the people, can help in this problem that is destroying our society. Acquire all the possible knowledge on drugs so you can help yourself avoid their consumption and thus you can help your children and others. We should inform others, especially the youth about the dangers and risks to those that are exposed to the consumption of drugs so that everyone can say no to drugs and preserve our generation so our civilization along with the human race can endure.

Other Vices: Gambling

The practice of gambling has occurred throughout history, as a recreational activity in the name of entertainment and diversion. In all societies, men have found gambling a source of pleasure during their free time, and even as a social medium. For more than 2,500 years before Christ, in the Middle East, China, India, and Egypt games like dominos, Parcheesi, and backgammon were played and we continue to play them today. It is believed that the Chinese were the first to introduce the formal game and in formulating its rules. Perhaps to add more interest to these games, betting appeared, but then due to the fact that this would cause disputes among the players for the payment of the debt acquired, the bets began to be controlled and even prohibited, something which has never been easy.

Gambling is characterized essentially by betting. In these games the possibilities of winning or losing do not depend much on the ability of the player but more on chance and possibility. Among the more popular gambling games are: dominos, dice, cards, lottery, slot machines, roulettes, etc. However, now Internet gambling sites, in their majority illegal, have added a new dimension to the cultural phenomenon of gambling. And according to some it has increased the problems derived from this vice exponentially. These games produce so much money that the proprietors of these web pages are contemplating using part of their proceeds to change the laws of the countries where they have their biggest markets and operate legally.

The majority of the people who gamble do not have any problem since it is done simply for enjoyment, but some people become addicted and lose control until the game becomes a problem. The addiction to gambling can dominate the life of an addictive person leading him to the loss of his values, relationships, job, and their grasp on their financial and familial obligations. The signs of addiction include: thinking constantly about gambling, lying about it, utilizing family or work time to gamble, feeling bad after playing but not stopping from doing it with money that is needed for other things. Just like addictions to drugs, compulsive gambling causes a sensation of euphoria when playing and discomfort, concern, or irritability when trying to interrupt the game.

5. How to Achieve a Full Life

In the previous chapter we covered the topics necessary for the development of the right attitude in life in order to allow us to make the difficult task of living easier. In this chapter we will go over the required steps for achieving happiness with the support of the subconscious mind so we can finally live a full life. Personal happiness, the level of satisfaction of needs and the aspirations in our lives, is intimately linked to our way of thinking, feeling, and seeing the world. In order to be happy, we must want it, then after satisfying our basic needs, we must begin to dream about our aspirations so we can move toward the path of prosperity and success. It is also necessary to overcome our fears, and to finally choose a good partner with whom to share our happiness.

In order to achieve happiness, a virtuous personality and the right attitude in life will undeniably help us. For everything else, we will rely on the power of the subconscious mind. Using the enormous power that we carry inside, we can manage to solve our problems, as well as, all that is necessary to achieve a full life. The only thing we have to do is to learn to program our subconscious and for this we only need to relax, connect the conscious with the subconscious, and ask for what we desire.

Now, what would happen if after achieving all the happiness in the world, we did not have a society in which to live a full life? We would then also need to turn our attention towards our society to make it more humane so we could all live life to the fullest and without problems. The happier the people we have around us, the greater the possibility there will be to heal the generation that will serve to conserve a more beautiful world.

5.1 Personal Happiness

Happiness is a state of mind that is produced in a person when he achieves a desired goal. This happiness generates joy and inner peace, a positive perspective on life that at the same time stimulates us to conquer new goals.

Personal happiness can be defined as the level of satisfaction of the needs and aspirations in the life of each person. It is intimately linked to our way of thinking, feeling, and seeing the world. In fact, just thinking positively makes us automatically feel happy.

In order to be happy, we must first desire it, and then fill our basic needs of food, clothing, shelter, and transportation. In order to satisfy these needs, we must work hard and fill them completely, never half way. After achieving these two fundamentals (wanting to be happy and filling our basic needs), we begin to dream about our aspirations, which will lead us to prosperity and success. Then, we must overcome our fears, and to complete this picture of happiness, we should choose a good partner with whom to share our wellbeing.

Having Aspirations: Factory of Dreams

In a survey that I took among women and men, young people and adults, to see what their aspirations were I surprisingly found that the majority of them did not give a definite response when asked about what they wanted most in life. I could feel that the majority of the people do not have aspirations, which is why they roam around life like weathervanes following whatever course the wind dictates. Life without aspirations is like a project without a plan. Without aspirations, there are no dreams.

When we dream about the things we want, that information reaches the subconscious mind, which is in charge of creating the necessary conditions for the dreams to become a reality. I remember I was 7 years old when I created my first dream. I had walked next to my mother close to 5 miles to go to another town more prosperous than ours to try and sell some fruits and thus being able to buy food for our family. After we managed to sell everything, we embarked on the trip back home through the same path. While I walked, I thought about how hard that activity was and that there should be a better way to get the daily sustenance. I dreamt that I could go to school and graduate as an engineer in order to help my mother and make her life much easier.

Thirty seven years later, already a prosperous man, and with four levels of education of the five existing ones, I returned to my home town to participate in an event for helping in the formation of a new school of higher education. A group of the town people, all professionals, including myself, was received by the mayor of the town, who was a contemporary of ours. He began his speech thanking us for our initiative in wanting to help the town people. He also said with much sadness that he would have liked to become a professional like us instead of a politician. He then said that the reason why he could not study was because he had no money. However; he then said, "There is someone here among you that was poorer than me, and I really don't know how he accomplished it." The mayor was talking about me. The difference between the mayor and me was our dreams.

Our dreams initiate us to the realization of our aspirations, reaching the knowledge of the tools necessary to produce the resources that we would be needed to be prosperous people and to continue our path towards total happiness

Being Prosperous

Prosperity consists of having that which we want and need to lead a life without economic anguishes. However, sometimes we see that even when a person makes enough money, he will not feel prosperous, which lead us to conclude that prosperity goes beyond just money. Prosperity should be seen as a mental state, and as such, it needs to be fed with positive thoughts in order to manifest itself.

A prosperous person manages to do more things with fewer resources. In other words, their income is always sufficient to cover their expenses, hence managing an economic situation that is adequate and healthy. Another important aspect of prosperity is abundance, which happens to be its cousin. The secret for always living in abundance is to share it. When we give something, our subconscious takes it as if we are doing well, since if we give; it is because we have something to give. This gives us a sensation of well-being, making the subconscious try to give us more to share since that is its function; making us feel good.

It is important to preserve the chain of giving and receiving. However, there are people that do not like to give, others that do not like to receive, and others that do not like to give or receive. Selfish people and vain people cannot be prosperous. In prosperity, everything flows and there is always abundance for everyone. Money begins to work in our favor instead of us working to obtain it. Also, to be prosperous, we must develop a sense of gratitude, which will open up the door to prosperity and abundance of life.

Another very important thing for obtaining prosperity is to have a positive attitude towards money, as we have seen in subchapter 4.5. If this attitude is positive, the person can become prosperous even if in his beginnings he had economic difficulties. In fact, 85% of prosperous people have had a difficult childhood or at the very least, had to make sacrifices. The habits acquired as a child forge the human being, tune him, give him and awaken in him, his strength and drive. Struggle causes them to develop an ability to manage abundance in the context of their own experience of scarcity. Prosperous people share their abundance with others, without bargaining it away. In general, these people live with much simplicity and wisdom. It would seem as if I were describing Mr. Antonio. In a few words, in order to be prosperous, it is necessary to be mentally prepared for it, have a positive attitude towards money, and share abundance.

Having Success

Having success means to achieve what is desired. This situation of triumph or achievement makes the person feel satisfied and experience happiness. Success can be planned or can happen spontaneously. Whichever the case, it is a product of our thoughts. Our thought molds our lives, which is why reaching success depends on our way of thinking. Once success is achieved, we can make other dreams a reality, which allows us at the same time to achieve our aspirations and be prosperous. Therefore, success depends exclusively on us.

The aspects, which are required for success, vary with respect to the aspirations of each person. For some people, to have success could mean to achieve an economic wellbeing, while for others it could be to have wisdom, and still others to find the love of their life and form a beautiful family. The most important thing about having success is simply for the person to feel happy with all he achieves. Now, to be successful, the person must possess certain qualities such as; having good self-esteem, being persistent, being willing to run certain risks in the endeavor he wishes to undertake, having the capacity to work with people, having certain talent, and feeling a passion for what he wants to do.

Feeling good about oneself or having positive self-esteem is essential not only for the achievement of success, but also for taking on any activity, which implies some risk. As we know, success is always associated with risk. As far as persistence goes, this is something that also requires intelligence in order to determine how far to persist in order to achieve what is desired. Another of the elements that is required to have success is to know how to work with people to achieve with them and through them the objective. For this, people can be just as important as money itself. To know the trade into which you want to venture and have the respective talent is also a necessary part for the achievement of what is pursued. Of course, when there is passion for what one wants then success is sweeter.

Success is tightly linked to seizing the opportunities that life presents us with. Now, for this to happen, we must always think positively, as this is what precisely marks the difference between achieving and not achieving success. Also, in order to have success, we must have the will to achieve it, have a positive attitude in life, create our dreams, and work to achieve our aspirations.

Overcoming Fears

As we have seen in the section about fear of subchapter 3.2 on emotions, real or rational fear helps us act in time to an anticipated threat. In this case, this type of fear is positive. However, another type of fear exists that is very negative and only causes us problems. This is called irrational fear, a fear that we imagine. Among these fears, we have the fear of fear, of failure, not having money, getting old, death, and the worst of all, the fear of speaking in front of a group of people.

Irrational fear almost always is disproportionate with respect to the threat and can be very perturbing at the moment of a treat confrontation. This fear can freeze and paralyze us. To avoid this situation and deal with the fear effectively at the time it presents itself, it is recommended to breathe deeply various times, inhaling the air until the abdomen is full and exhaling it until it contracts. This process of breathing helps to oxygenate the cells in the body, which stimulates the stabilization of the mind.

To obtain personal happiness and achieve a full life, we must overcome irrational fears. For this, we must first admit that we are afraid, then we have to identify the fear to better understand it, and finally to confront it in order to overcome it. To accept or identify fear is important, since it permits us to observe if there is any manifestation associated with it, such as a tendency to evade situations, or feelings of palpitations, sensations of having butterflies in the stomach, sweating, or dry mouth. Once the fear is identified, we must try to understand it in order to control it.

To understand fear is to know its cause or root better so that the necessary changes needed to overcome it are possible. This comprehension allows us to detect if the fear comes from experiences, teachings, stereotypes they have tagged us with, or any aspect of our personality. To confront fear is to do precisely what we fear the most. Eventually fear becomes mundane and the frightfulness disappears. If fear is the result of uncertainty about the future or of what happened in the past, we only need to live in the present to overcome this fear.

A point of great importance for overcoming fears is to generate more positive thoughts since irrational fear is produced by negative thoughts. Positive thinking stabilizes the mind, which helps us see the situation in a better way. To achieve this objective it is necessary to eliminate negative thoughts and cultivate positive thinking, as we mentioned before. Now, to make this change in our thinking we need to reprogram our mind in the way discussed in subchapter 5.3.

If with our aspirations, we have achieved prosperity and success and have also managed to overcome our fears, then we should feel happy. Now, to be happier, we must choose a good partner with whom we can share all that happiness. It is important to know that a good relationship should always provide more happiness than the person had before the relationship.

Choosing a Good Partner

In the majority of developed societies, people still have the liberty to share their life with someone they love. The relationship between couples is based on love; a universal feeling that has existed since the beginning of humanity. To fall in love is something very normal for a human being. That arrow shot that we feel that first time we see someone that we really like, is a one-time emotional occurrence which should be followed with a reciprocal acknowledgement between the two people. In that moment the brain releases certain hormones, like dopamine, among others, which prepares the body to manage that great emotion.

Falling in love initiates the construction of true love. In the beginning, everything is based on friendship and later with affection, compassion, and tenderness, love begins to strengthen. It reaches a point in the relationship that the couple loves each other so much that they decide to live together and start formalizing the union. However, living under the same roof, and getting under the same covers, means to share intimacy. This can sometimes not be easy, but thanks to the magic of love, people adapt to their new circumstances. Being in love, transforms the life of people so much, that they act like if they had taken a strong dose of concentrated happiness. They see the world as more beautiful, they do things with more affection, and they love themselves and others more. The explanation to all these changes is that the chemical that the brain generates while it is falling in love makes the mind generate many more positive thoughts. If this is the case, then let's continue falling in love!

To remain in love with our partner, it is important to have made a good selection when choosing them. For this, it is necessary to know what type of person we want to share our life with. Generally, when we feel attracted to a person, it is because they have the qualities that we desire. People in general look for a partner that is nice, comprehensive, intelligent, honest, emotionality stable, attractive, and healthy. However, cultures determine the importance that is attributed to each of these qualities. Men mainly give more importance to the youth and physical attraction of their partners, important qualities in terms of fertility. Women, on the other hand, generally prefer men that have a decent social and economic status, or at least have enough potential to acquire these positions; and also prefer men that are a few years older than them.

The qualities that a person wants from another person should be the ones that normally determine the decision to get together so that the life they share can be compatible. By not following the guidelines of the qualities desired, the rupture in the union is inevitable. The problem with this norm is that the majority of the people do not know what qualities they desire and only use their heart as a guide for selecting their partner. As a general rule and without realizing it much, we choose our partners based on the model, provided by our parents, whether good or bad. Our love towards them causes us see them as the template to follow as a guide to pattern our behavior, which is why when the time comes for choosing a partner; we do it based on this. Generally, men would pick their partner based on how much she looked like their mother, while women picked them in relation to their father.

This could function if the model we obtained from our mother or father was good, but what if this was not the case? Suppose that your mother was submissive and lived all her life with your father putting up with all his mistreatments and dishonesty only to continue with a life she believed she could not confront alone. Would you like to repeat this type of life? Clearly, the answer is no. The importance of the norm of desired qualities comes to light. However, the majority of the people do not apply this rule perhaps because of their lack of knowledge or for not giving it the importance it merits.

Generally, only desirable people can attract people as equally desirable as them. Our partner should be compatible with us. Intelligent and educated people tend to marry people with whom they can share their ideas and wisdom. Attractive and seductive people look for a partner as equally attractive and seductive. People with opposite qualities rarely attract each other. Choosing a good partner in order to preserve the union and guarantee that the subsequent generation is part of the natural selection of our evolutionary process.

For the union between couples to last, it is necessary that good communication exist between them so they can resolve the differences that come about throughout the relationship. It is worth mentioning, that daily problems should be resolved as soon as possible during that same day. Do not let them accumulate since that will only wear out the relationship. It is important to talk and listen to the other person to try and understand them. When someone feels that their partner pays them attention and understands them, this motivates them to tell them everything, well, almost everything. Good communication includes expressing your feelings, concerns, and projects, as well as, being receptive to the opinion that the other person may have in respect to it.

Being honest is fundamental for a relationship to last. I remember that one of my best disciples told me that he wanted to divorce his wife because he had fallen in love with another woman and that it would be dishonest if he didn't. To which I said. "My dear friend, your problem is being weak. It is normal for one to like the beautiful girls he sees daily, but it is a weakness to fall in love with them to try to replace the woman that we already have at home and thus throw out the window everything we have constructed with love over time: our family, with a wife and children." We also see that besides being honest and respectful, we need to also be firm when faced with temptation, just like Jesus was on his walk through the desert for forty days and forty nights.

There should likewise be a common respect and courtesy between couples. We all like to be treated with affection, tolerance, consideration, and above all, respect. Spontaneously telling our partner that we love them is a small way to demonstrate this, yet at the same time an immense way of showing love. We should please our partner in everything we possibly can. In fact, that is what love is all about; trying to make someone happy. As far as respect, this is so important that no relationship can survive without it. Raising your voice to your partner is a lack of respect. Hitting your partner is sufficient reason to separate. Respect also leads us to being tolerant and considerate with our partner.

Another key aspect in a relationship between couples is the trust that exists between them. A healthy relationship should last until trust ends. The members of the couple should be able to open themselves up without the other one trying to exert any control as long as, what he or she does is not detrimental to the relationship. Distrust is a product of bad thoughts that cause insecurity and jealousy, but at this stage in the book, those thoughts will no longer be a problem, since we have already seen how to resolve them.

For the relationship to develop and grow, it is important that the leader always be the one to generate the better thoughts and the one that is the most productive, of course. The couple should take advantage of sharing a lot while the circumstances allow it. Socializing with friends and family is desirable. Enjoying time together will add a pinch of emotion to the life of the couple. Every now and then, to do one of the crazy things they used to do at the beginning of the relationship, adds a touch of fire back to the union.

Once the conjugal rules of the union are followed and the relationship is stable and you have enjoyed about 5 years of happiness with your partner, you can then start thinking about having children. If people marry at 27 years old like they should, by the time they have their first child, they should already have reached a level of maturity requisite for raising a child. To avoid the surprise of some good parents, when they see with sadness that their children did not come out like them, they should supervise the upbringing of their children. Some parents concentrate so much in providing the necessary economic resources so their family lacks nothing that they forget this small detail.

Well... With the development of the right attitude in life, it is easier to walk through it in search of a better living and with the achievement of personal happiness we can then live fully. Many of the things that we need to reach this point, we have covered in the book. However, there are some things that depending on the attitude that the person has already developed, takes a bit more to understand and much more to change. For this reason, I have included the topic of the subconscious mind to help us achieve those things, which are harder to reach.

5.2 The Power of the Subconscious Mind

Inside the subconscious mind resides an infinite intelligence capable of leading us to achieve everything we desire in life. For this to be possible, we should have knowledge of the interaction of our conscious mind with the subconscious, with which we can modify our way of thinking. Besides, we should be open minded and receptive people to accept any new thought or idea. This is fundamental in achieving any other necessary element for living a full life.

The subconscious mind is the one that dictates to us what to do. The reason why the use of the power of the subconscious mind to achieve the things we want had not been generalized before has been because of the total lack of knowledge on how this marvel functions. Ah, but once we manage to decipher its functioning, then we will be able to put all its power under our control and thus, be able to change our lives in order to be happier. We can make the power of our subconscious help us instead of going against us, which usually happens in some situations.

While the conscious mind generates the instructions for the execution of our daily tasks, the subconscious mind stores information obtained from feelings, emotions, and the thoughts of the day. Our subconscious mind works all the time. It is something extraordinarily wonderful even when the majority of the people do not know what it is, nor how it functions, but at least they know it exists. There are many ways in which people using the conscious mind can influence the subconscious, but most people do not know how to do it since generally the conscious mind is not aware of what the subconscious mind does. These two levels in the mind can work together, but not always be in agreement. Now, when they enter into a conflict, the subconscious always wins.

The conscious mind functions like a computer, which retains the information that we programmed into it and can only, interpret that information literally.

Something similar occurs with the subconscious, since it does not know the difference between reality and imagination. When we think or talk internally to ourselves, our subconscious stores in its memory this information as a real act and makes it produce the necessary conditions for the event related to the thought to execute according to how we have programmed it.

What the subconscious mind does will depend on the programming that we put into it, which signifies that we can control it so that it can help us achieve good things. Generally, we program our subconscious mind each day while we think about what we will do. If we think it will go well, then it will go well. It is that simple! We are what we think. We will have success in our life if our thoughts are positive. With this type of thinking we can confront adverse situations no matter how serious they are and achieve our goals.

With negative thoughts, failure is the only thing pursued. Without realizing it we program our subconscious to allow that type of situation, and every time we have to confront it, that negative thought will appear to make us fail. However, today, when we have entered into the subconscious mind we have discovered that just like we are able to program bad thoughts, we can also deprogram or change them, into positive ones. In order to achieve this it is important to understand that the feelings and emotions, like behavior, when confronting a situation, are a result of our thoughts and these are simply ideas not reality. With this in mind, we can initiate ourselves in the learning of how to program our subconscious.

5.3 Programming the Subconscious Mind

In order to program the subconscious, our mind should be very relaxed and functioning at a minimum rhythm, but still conscious. This is known as Alpha level. At this level, the conscious can connect with the subconscious to send a message regarding what it wants to achieve. To reach the Alpha level, it is important to know the levels of consciousness and follow the guidelines recommended here to reach the Alpha. *We program the subconscious with affirmations and visualizations that we pass from the level of the conscious mind to the subconscious while we are in the Alpha level.*

Since the subconscious does not know how to distinguish between past, present and future, neither between the imaginary and the real, the subconscious will believe that what is affirmed and visualized is real. Then it will create all the required routes to achieve what we have put in it. When the affirmations and visualizations pass from the conscious to the subconscious, the message is sent and ready for execution.

The Preparations for Programming

The subconscious mind records what the conscious mind prints on it. In other words, the subconscious mind accepts what the conscious creates without reasoning and without entering into controversy. It is how the earth accepts any kind of seed, whether it is good, or bad. If the thoughts are positive, they can prosper in the form of good seeds. If they are negative they can produce adverse situations.

Even more, the subconscious mind does not even notice if the thoughts are true of false. For example, if someone firmly believes that something is true, even if it is false; his subconscious mind will accept it as true and will proceed to obtain results according to that acceptance. For this reason, it is very important to know what we think. Any thought, belief or assumption that we imagine, remains recorded in our subconscious mind and later that thought, belief, or assumption tries to manifest itself in the form of circumstances, conditions, and events in our lives. For these mental manifestations to be good, we should feed the subconscious with positive thoughts.

To program the subconscious, our mind should be very relaxed in the Alpha level. In other words, functioning at a minimum rhythm, where the electrical impulses of the brain oscillate at a speed of approximately 10 cycles per minute. It is very important to know that we pass through the Alpha level every day before falling asleep at night and when we begin to awaken in the morning. However, to reach this level at any other moment in the day, we can utilize methods of relaxation and meditation. Once in Alpha, we begin to program the subconscious utilizing mental affirmations and visualizations.

Affirmations and Visualizations

As we have already said, our subconscious does not know how to distinguish between the past, present, and future, nor between the imaginary and the real. It is very important to have this in mind to understand why we utilize affirmations and visualizations in the programming of the subconscious mind.

Affirmations are declarations that are made of oneself at any time about how one is and how one wants to be. If we affirm to ourselves that we are completely quiet and content while we are in this Alpha level, our subconscious will receive the message and find the necessary conditions to take us to that state of mind even if in reality we feel anxious and depressed. Our subconscious will believe in what we affirm to it.

Visualizations are mental images that are created about oneself achieving anything that one wants to do or be. When we visualize, we really dream while awake, since we imagine step by step in detail how things happen or how we will achieve the things we want. Like the subconscious believes that what it visualizes is real, then it will create all the required routes to achieve what is wanted. For this, affirmations as well as, visualizations should pass whether through the form of a message or any other way to the subconscious mind.

Sending Messages to the Subconscious

We can program our subconscious mind through the sending of messages from the conscious mind. To send messages, we must first reach the Alpha level where we will be totally relaxed, but also completely conscious. At this point it is possible to connect the conscious with the subconscious and send messages from into the latter. These messages are reinforced through mental affirmations and visualizations. With these messages, we can tell the subconscious what we want to be and make the changes that are needed to achieve it.

We can use these messages to tell our subconscious to help us change our thoughts, better our health, overcome our fears, have success, or any other thing we want to achieve. It is a privilege to have access to this astounding power of the subconscious to achieve things that would be impossible to achieve any other way. However, that power is nothing new since it has been with us for thousands of years. The most difficult thing about the process is to achieve the Alpha level and to make it easier; we should understand the different levels of consciousness.

Levels of Consciousness

Our cerebral activity depends on what our body is doing at a determined moment of the day or night. According to the activity of our brain, we experience various levels of consciousness each day. These levels are defined by the rhythm with which the cerebral waves are vibrating. There exist four primary levels of consciousness through which all people pass through every day. These levels are known as: Beta, Alpha, Theta, and Delta.

Beta Level

We are in this conscious level when our brain registers an activity of 14 or more cycles per second. The majority of us are at this level for more than 70% of our time. Beta is the level of the conscious mind where we think rationally to achieve the activities of the day, which is why we are always awake, alert, and conscious of our 5 senses and of making decisions. The left side of the brain dominates in the Beta level.

Alpha Level

In the Alpha level, our brain registers an activity between 7-14 cycles per second. The Alpha level is the creative one. We are in the Alpha level when we are daydreaming or when we are relaxed and sleepy but conscious. Every day before we fall asleep or completely wake up, we pass through the Alpha level. The right part of the brain dominates in alpha, which is the intuitive level instead of the rational one. From the Alpha level, solutions can be received to solve problems that present themselves in the

Beta level. Alpha is the level of consciousness where we can access our subconscious so it can help us resolve all our problems.

Theta Level

In the Theta level of consciousness, our brain registers an activity between 4-7 cycles per seconds. In this level the majority of the people sleep. However, with practice one can learn to remain passively conscious in this level of consciousness to achieve extraordinary powers of mind control and obtain extrasensory perceptions. If we could program our subconscious while we are in the Theta level, solving problems would be much easier and more effective than in the Alpha level.

Delta Level

In this level, the activity registered by our brain is below 4 cycles per second. In Delta, we are all in a deep sleep and totally unconscious.

How Do We Reach the Alpha Level?

Many ways exist to reach the Alpha level. You can use the one that results easier for you. Following, we present step by step, one of the simplest methods:

> 1. <u>An appropriate place</u>. Choose a place that is alone and very silent, preferably in your house, free of interruptions or distractions where you feel the most comfortable. You can sit vertically with

your feet on the floor and your hands on your knee with the palms upward or you can lie down on your back with your arms parallel to your body. In whichever position you choose, you should close your eyes, try not to cross your legs, and assure yourself that your spine is straight. You should feel comfortably balanced.

2. Relaxation. Tense your muscles as tightly as you can from your head to your to your feet and then allow them to loosen up. The difference between the tension that is felt when we tensed our muscles and the calm that is felt when they are loosened, give you a point of reference for the sensation of relaxation. Now, to completely relax, we should breathe appropriately.

3. Breathing. Breathe deeply, inhaling air through the nose and exhaling it through the mouth, concentrating on the entrance and exit of air. Breathe through your diaphragm so the area of the stomach moves up and down. In normal breathing, the oxygen that is inhaled is perfectly balanced with the carbon dioxide that is exhaled maintaining the pH of your blood balanced. Breathe appropriately using all your lung capacity, holding the air for a while and then exhaling it all through the mouth. In this way, the lungs extract more oxygen from the air to put in the bloodstream.

4. <u>Count Backwards</u>. Once you have completely relaxed, count from 10 to 1 to reach the Alpha level. It is possible that at the beginning you may have to start counting from 17 until you have the necessary practice.

5. <u>Visualization</u>. Once in the Alpha, visualize a mental image about a place where you feel very relaxed. Imagine that place very vividly in your mind with all its details. A place with trees, flowers, birds, and clear water with the smell of the forest is always very relaxing. While you are in this peaceful and tranquil place, your senses will be alert; knowing everything that is happening around you and you will be able to totally concentrate on the thoughts that come spontaneously into your mind. Envision yourself very calm and serene inside this place of peace and tranquility. Take a mental image of the peace that you feel in this place so you can visualize it again later when you feel tense. To leave the Alpha level, just stop visualizing your place of peace and tranquility and open your eyes.

5.4 How to Ask our Subconscious

We can ask our subconscious to help us with whatever we need to be happy, to solve problems, to make any changes in our way of thinking, achieve things, to better our economic status, in all; we can ask for anything we want. To achieve this, we can use various ways for passing from the conscious mind to the subconscious the information about what is desired. One of these ways is to send a message to our subconscious while we are in the alpha level, where it is possible to connect the conscious with the subconscious.

We can also ask the subconscious through prayer, which should connect the conscious with the subconscious in order to be effective, in the same way that Jesus used it. Prayer is the harmonious interaction of the two levels of the mind, the conscious and the subconscious, directed towards a specific purpose. We can meditate to reach the Alpha level like we did in the previous section. Once in the alpha, we pray, giving thanks to our subconscious or to God for all the accomplishments of the day, and then we specifically ask for what we want and how we want it. Finally, we mentally visualize the entire process of the achievement of what we have asked for.

For example, suppose you want to ask the subconscious to help you have a new car since the one you already have is too old with too many issues, and you are not earning the sufficient money for the monthly payments of a new automobile. Your prayer could go something like this; "I want to give thanks to my subconscious for all the accomplishments of today, like having seen my daughter that I had not seen in 7 days. I would also like to thank my subconscious for the recuperation of my aunt after her surgery. Now, I would like to ask my subconscious to help me buy a new car since the one I have is not functioning correctly and I need it for work and for transporting my family".

Now begin to visualize the accomplishment of your petition. Imagine you are going to your job and visualize the whole route you normally take to get to work. Imagine that after being at your job, your boss calls you and tells you that the company has decided to give you a raise for your good work. Visualize your walk to your boss, his office with all the possible details, the words and the face of your boss giving you the news and of course, visualize the happiest face, even your own, thanking your boss. Later, visualize your return home and giving the good news. Visualize your happiness and the happiness of your family. You can repeat this operation up to three times if you wish to be assured that the information has passed from the conscious to the subconscious.

If you do not have the time at your disposal or you don't want to go through the process of reaching the Alpha level, then you can do it before falling asleep at night or before waking up in the morning. Remember that every day before we fall asleep or completely wake up, we pass through the Alpha level. Then, once you are relaxed and ready to go to sleep, initiate your prayer with all its visualization. Repeat it until you fall asleep. This will be a sign that the message has passed to the subconscious. Say the prayer all the days that it is necessary. If at any moment of the day your petition comes to mind, reinforce it with positive thoughts.

Once we have achieved - with the help of our subconscious mind - the other necessary things for living a full life, it is important also that the society which we form a part of, is conditioned for making possible the full enjoyment of life. For this reason, we should know our society of which we are part of, which is why we should not isolate ourselves from it.

5.5 A Better Society

Today's society is found somewhat divided to the point that each person walks his own way pretending to have his own rules. We live in a society, which with the passing of time has been accruing many social problems like drugs, delinquency, corruption, and terrorism, among others. Perhaps the saddest thing is to know that our youth are also protagonists of some of these problems. It is believed that the root of the majority of the problems could be social maladjustment, which puts people on the margin of social normality becoming marginal. Confronted with the magnitude of these social problems, it is sad to accept the total apathy that reigns, not only in governments but also in society itself.

We see that instead of putting education at the service of people, they are using it for the purpose of politically indoctrinating the people, and that is not just. Education should be used for the imparting of knowledge to an individual so he can resolve his problems through a better way of thinking. As well as, imparting knowledge about the culture; the values like honesty, respect, and responsibility, and the guidelines of behavior so the individual can insert himself into society, lessening the possibility of social maladjustment, alienated from social problems. In this way, education will be part of the solution. The other part of the solution would consist in making changes ourselves to help others.

Today's Society

A great part of our society is sliding into the wrong path. The members of that part of society isolate themselves each time more and more and pretend to live alienated from the world. This isolation has been fragmenting society, producing a collective composed of individuals only. Each one walks his own way, pretending to have his own set of rules. The common values, as well as, sound customs, are no longer shared. Affection, respect, and the empathy for others, are being lost. Even worst, we are losing what makes a person human. It is sad to see in a great part of our compatriots, the fading of the critical elements for the development of a good attitude in life. Even sadder still is to see that social malady is now proliferating throughout the whole world.

This dangerous trend is not good for our society, since it is making people feel very confused, which generates chaotic situations. These people live today as if they were going to die tomorrow. This is making people less capable of thinking with clarity, paying attention, and concentrating, in order to solve their everyday problems. They become very dependent on someone else and wait for others to solve their problems, thus surges the messianic culture. In other words, believing that others will solve their problems. Some experts believe that the main reason for this situation is due to the political and economic instability of the countries in the world.

Besides this problem of isolation, we see that in the society we live in, with the passing of time, the social problems like drugs, delinquency, corruption, and terrorism, among many, have been increasing. The reason is simply due to the increase in unemployment in a great part of the world, which constantly pushes upward the level of poverty. However, it is curious to hear; now more than ever, politicians promise the people in order to win the elections, that they will end poverty. By the results we see, when you hear someone speak like this, you better get far away from him because for sure he will make you poorer so you will have to depend on his government and thus continue voting for him. Playing with poverty to obtain political benefit is an aberration.

When confronted with this desolate panorama, many people think that it is better not to get involved since it is quieter, and dedicate themselves to doing nothing, just watch TV. This makes the remedy worse than the sickness. Through TV they try to mire the brain of the people and impose on them strange ideas that are not compatible with the majority of today's society. Now they even want to destroy the family, the foundation of our society, with deviated practices on how the constitution of the family should be. This is something very different than from how it has always been: a mother, a father and children.

On the other hand, we see with a lot of worry and much aggression in the youth. Aggressive young people usually come from parents that, besides not paying enough attention to them, disciplined them too harshly creating in them strong traumas that end up diminishing their empathetic ability and filling them with hate towards other people. For sure, these young problematic people will be the propagators of violence and crime in our society. Their scarce capacity to control themselves contributes to their being bad students and incapable of making friends. Feeling that they have no friends, they join other social outcasts to form groups and defy the law. They become consumers of alcohol and drugs. Others also feeling marginalized are attracted by their defiant style to join those groups.

These outcasts are young people that lack complete supervision in their homes and have begun to roam through the streets liberally during their elementary school years. Later, during their junior high education, this group of outcasts tends to abandon school slipping into delinquency and thus becoming antisocial. Of course, this is not the only road to antisocial behavior. There are many other factors for example, being born in a neighborhood with a high crime rate or coming from a family with high levels of stress and poverty.

Social Problems

Perhaps the root of almost all the known social problems could be not being able to socially adapt since this problem generally leads to drugs, corruption, delinquency, and terrorism. This of course entails other problematic situations that currently confront society, like the abandonment of the home by adolescents, and prostitution especially in very young girls. The apathy of society could also be contributing to these social problems.

The problems previously mentioned, can be common since we have heard about them since a long time ago. However, the unusual thing is to hear that some politicians have recruited common delinquents to corrupt them and thus have them corrupt others to gain some political benefit. If for some reason, the corruption fails, then they appeal to terrorism with less scrupulous delinquents. It appears that nothing detains these people and they run over anybody that stands in their way of achieving their misdeeds. Far from helping solve social problems, what they do is stimulate them more.

Social Non-adaptability

Social non-adaptability is the incapability of a person to adapt to the conditions and conducts of the society where he lives and develops. People who find themselves in a situation of social non-adaptability put themselves on the margin of social normality, manifesting a behavior that totally disagrees with the prevailing social norms. These individuals become marginal people.

Among the causes of social non-adaptability can be the problems in the family nucleus like abuse and child abandonment by the parents. It could also be caused by the beliefs of a person not compatible with the society they form a part of. Another cause that can lead to non-adaptability is bad company, which is also very common among adolescents. Non-adaptability is a social problem, perhaps the root of the major social problems that has been experienced in all societies around the world.

Drugs

In the majority of cases of alcoholism or consumers of drugs, the beginning of the addiction could be in their adolescent years even though not all who try drugs end up alcoholics or drug addicts. Addiction requires, apart from trying the drug for the first time, other factors like the place and environment where you live and the emotional aspect of the individual. If a young person lives in a neighborhood where drug use is rampant, he runs the risk of being a drug addict. Besides, generally children of drug addicts tend to be more vulnerable to the addiction.

As far as the emotional aspect, young people who are more susceptible to become addicts are those that have a higher index of emotional disturbances. The most emotionally unstable people seem to find in drugs, a way of calming the emotions that trouble them; while, other people are led to drugs by their state of depression. However, the effects of alcohol often worsen the depression after the brief euphoria. People with drug and alcohol problems should seek help in institutions like Alcoholics Anonymous and other programs for recovery as soon as possible.

Corruption

People who are unable to adapt to society don't care about anything. They do anything they can to infringe upon the law and cause harm to society. They bribe, extort, use fraud, and the traffic of any influence they can have to corrupt someone and thus obtain some economic benefit. This action and effect of corrupting is called corruption, which has become an enormous social problem since it destroys the foundations of society.

It is believed that people who were unable to adapt to society, brought the corruption to the political sector, when they managed to occupy a political position. Then after this, they extended it to the private sector, contaminating every stratum of everyday life. The reason for the enormous proliferation of corruption was the indifference in resolving the problem by the governments themselves with the silence of the people as an accomplice. Each day that passes, the solutions to corruption drift further away since this social cancer infests society more and more which will definitely make it more difficult to eradicate.

Today, corruption affects not only the social, but also all the aspects of society in any part of the world. In the political world, it harms democratic institutions by distorting the electoral processes. Today, we know of politicians who have bribed citizens without caring about class or position to win an election. In the economic sector, corruption has a negative effect on the economic development of any country by slowing the economy driving away investments, and without them we cannot create resources for employment. The scourge of corruption completely destabilizes countries and regions.

Delinquency
Delinquency is the conduct that results from the failures of a person to adapt to the demands of the society in which he lives. Juvenile delinquency is one of the most important social problems in the world today and if it is not attended to now, it will become the adult delinquency of tomorrow.

A juvenile delinquent is a person not adapted to society, impulsive, and aggressive perhaps with the desire for prominence, and who drags in his short life, a chain of failures. Besides this, he consumes drugs, has low self-esteem, and comes from a low-income family with many problems. To help these young people there are programs in some places directed to the prevention of juvenile delinquency. Governments and society itself should try to help these young people in order to preserve the integrity of the family since this is the foundation of society. If common delinquency is not taken care of in time, it will end up forming part of organized crime, which could lead to terrorism.

Terrorism

People who are not able to adapt and are impulsive and aggressive with very profound beliefs in a religious cause develop an exaggerated fanaticism about a determined doctrine or dogma. These people generally come to practice criminal acts in organized gangs to indiscriminately infuse terror in society with political or religious intentions, which is known as terrorism.

Terrorists do not understand that their beliefs are something very personal and not universal, so as to pretend to impose them on the rest of the world through force. This has been perhaps their great error for so long. Terrorist are dogmatic people with a very negative point of view towards society and who perceive the world as something bad that needs to be eliminated, it is for this reason they see other people with different ideologies as their enemies who have to be exterminated somehow.

By infusing terror and fear in people, terrorism creates chaos and insecurity in society, destabilizing it as well as its governments. Terrorism is a complex problem that is affecting many parts of our lives since it is tightly linked to drugs and indoctrination, which normally goes against the good and sound practices of society. Today we see terrorism converted into the armed wing of drug trafficking and of politicians to achieve criminal recklessness.

Total Apathy

Sometimes it is hard to understand how people can make themselves deaf and blind to the problems of others especially of the youth. Today, we assume a comfortable position of not doing anything. It seems that what we yesterday called a rare issue has now become the norm. All of us as a group form part of society and what affects it also affects us.

We see with sadness that street children almost always end up consuming drugs and later becoming delinquents without anyone doing something in respect to it. This problem in its initial stage could have been solved, but once advanced when the delinquent has already become a threat to society, rehabilitation is more difficult. The small problem has already complicated and has passed from street vandalism to organized crime and no one wants to do anything. We see then that the apathy is total.

To top it off, governments now, instead of confronting their responsibility, try to elude it like water, choosing the path of least resistance. Governments, faced with the problem of drugs, are legalizing it while touting the benefits of tax revenues. If you are held up in the streets, they will tell you that it is your fault for being there and if you refer to your attacker as illegal, terrorist, etc. they will accuse you of being politically incorrect. How about that? The apathy of people towards people, of society towards people, and of government towards society, adds up to total apathy.

Education

We see with much sadness and worry that education instead of being put to the service of the people, is being used for the means of politically indoctrination to the masses through the imposition of behaviors contrary to good and sound customs, as well as, the imposition of economic models that have proven to be failures in the past, submerging a lot of people into total poverty. That is not fair.

Education should be defined as the process of imparting knowledge to an individual so he can develop his mental and physical capacities with the purpose of being able to solve the problems that will present themselves in the course of his life. In this way and through this knowledge imparted about culture; values like honesty, respect, and responsibility; as well as, the guidelines of behavior attached to sound customs; the individual would be in a better position to solve his problems, adapt, and fully integrate into the society in which he lives and develops.

To achieve this purpose, education should include teachings on how the human body functions to better understand our physical abilities and limitations, as well as, how to keep it healthy. We should also teach how the human mind functions to understand the mental processes that are produced inside, especially everything related to emotions and thoughts. With the knowledge of thinking, we learn not only to think, but also to think the right way. In other words: in a logical, positive, and creative way. All the problems that plague humanity today have been caused by not having an adequate approach to thought. It is therefore, logical to think that in order to resolve our problems, we must change our thinking for one that is more profound.

The objective of all education should consist in managing to help people see one transcendent reality, not one invented for the convenience of certain groups. Teaching, as part of education, requires an exceptional communication skill to achieve the imparting of knowledge required to provide a person with the abilities, attitudes, and values necessary that will permit him to handle himself and solve the problems that present themselves in his everyday life.

The educational process should produce the necessary changes so the individual can confront his next goal with success. As the individual resolves his problems, the collective, whether it is the city, state or nation, will in the same way and in time, be resolving theirs. In elementary school, education should foster the interaction and co-existence between children and teachers. In high school, education should touch upon the aspects of thinking which will allow adolescents to think logically, positively, and creatively. In college, education should give the adults the necessary tools to achieve success and prosperity in order to lead a happy life. Educations should definitely be part of the solution.

The Solution

As we all know, the cabin of an airplane is pressurized through the pumping of compressed air so the passengers can breathe normally with the adequate level of oxygen and thus maintain an environment and an atmospheric pressure similar to when on land. If the cabin were not pressurized, the passengers would suffer from headaches and earaches, circulatory problems, fainting, and in extreme cases even death due to the fact that the plane rapidly ascends and the atmospheric pressure varies dramatically depending on the altitude.

Let's imagine that we are on a plane and a disturbance occurs in the cabin. In the demonstration that they normally do before takeoff they have given us instructions on what to do; "In case of a depressurization in the cabin, all the compartments on top of the seats that contain oxygen masks will open. If this should happen, quickly grab the oxygen mask, place it over the nose and mouth and breathe normally. The passengers that are traveling with children should place their masks on first and then proceed to place their child's."

I believe the analogy is appropriate to what is happening today in respect to the problem in our society that depressurizes more and more each day and makes it appear that oxygen is lacking and that this is making us do all types of stupid things. The other interesting part of the analogy is the solutions proposed to the problem. Using a very logical thought they instruct the passengers to put on the oxygen mask first. That is exactly what we should do in order to find the solution to the problems in our society. We have to start by making the necessary changes first in us, the adults, so we can then help our children.

Only when we manage to develop deeper thinking, learn to be emotionally intelligent, and assume the right attitude towards life, in other words, when we start to see life under a new perspective; only then, will we be able to help others so together we can resolve all of these problems. At this time, it is appropriate to remind you that all the problems that we have today as individuals or as a society have been created by our way of thinking. Which is why it is logical to assume that the solutions to our problems has to start by developing deeper thinking just like Albert Einstein expressed once when he said, "The problems we have today can only be solved with deep thinking".

It is time to start seeing our world with a higher vision. We have to detach ourselves from that enormous mental laziness that surrounds us so we can be more creative and productive and honor that group of human beings that came before us many years ago and that thanks to their thinking brought us to where we are today. It is time to wake up. It does not matter if what happens to us is what happened to Leonardo Da Vinci, who after doing so realized that he had awakened to see that the rest of the world slept.

We should wake up to appreciate, reflect, and defend the great legacy of Thomas Jefferson, one of the founding fathers of the United States, and a great thinker at the service of humanity. In his Declaration of Independence, which served to inspire many other countries, he held to the fact that we were all created equal, without any distinction, and that we all have the right to live, be free and be happy. This is the product of a very advanced thinking, which we should preserve for the good of all humanity in order to have governments of the people, by the people, and for the people like Abraham Lincoln said, another great thinker.

The hope of the world today is placed in the people that are awakening. Join this group of people for the pride of the new generation that will follow. To do this, you simply have to trade your way of thinking for a logical, positive, and creative one so it can help you grow, be happy, and help others. This thinking should be free from any ties and should always be for the service of personal good and the common good. In other words, a deeper thinking with which you will be able to recognize a good leader when he appears and follow him.

How great it would be, if one of those that had awakened would become an influential leader in the direction of the world. As of today, almost all the rulers have the same way of thinking that their predecessors did, which led us into so many problems. Ah! Some of them even speak to us about change but only manage to worsen the situation. The reason is that they don't have this deeper thinking for they have not yet awakened. The change they talk about is for the worst. Politicians with those conventional thoughts will never guide the world through the correct path.

The new generations each day have fewer possibilities of having a stable and prosperous life unless things change, but...who will change them? All the authorities that the people have elected to protect them have failed. They have all failed from the mayor's office, congresses, chiefs of state, and even world organizations that are supposedly at the service of humanity. Now, do you still believe those authorities could function one day?

Remember that those authorities are elected with the vote of the people, in places where it possible, but if each subsequent generation has less ability to know what is good or bad, how can it be electing brilliant authorities? Simply, they will continue voting for those that others indicate to them or for the ones who offer them a free lunch. The only way to produce any change in this perverse political tendency in society is by us changing, us, the people.

It would seem that we are alone. It is only us, the people, and us alone, who can make the changes that we need to rescue our society and our beautiful world that is slipping through our fingers. Yes, we can do it ourselves! As each one of us resolves his personal problems to live better, in that same measure, the society of which he forms part of, will also resolve its problems so that we can all live fully. The real revolution comes from the bottom up.

About The Author

Ivanni Delgado is an engineering graduate from the University of Tulsa, Oklahoma with a master in business from the University of NSU of Talehquah, Oklahoma. He currently directs an important company in the petroleum service industry. He has constantly been observing and analyzing the attitude of people with whom he works or relates to. He thinks that for a company to be productive, its people have to also be productive, which requires having an adequate attitude about what they do and that definitely will depend on their way of thinking. He has the particularity of turning any relationship, including work and business ones, into friendships. Like any good friend, he is given to helping others, and because of this he decided to write this book with the idea of helping people in the difficult task of living.

Bibliography

1. Calle, R. Guía Practica De La Salud Emocional, Spain: Edaf, 1998

2. Eades, M., M.D. The Doctor's Complete Guide to Vitamins and Minerals. New York: Dell. 2000

3. Goleman, D. Emotional Intelligence. New York: Bantam Books. 1997

4. Handly, R. Anxiety & Panic Attacks. Fawcett Crest: New York. 1985

5. Harrison, A. and Bramson, R., Ph.D. The Art of Thinking. New York: Berkley Books. 2002

6. Leahy, R., Ph.D. The Worry Cure. New York: Harmony Books. 2005

7. Murphy, J. The Power of Your Subconscious Mind. New York: Bantam Books. 2001